" WHEN YOU TRY OUT THESE REC...
THEY WILL REMIND YOU OF 'HOME' AND ..."

LOVE
Tommy, Frances & Family
xxx

AUG 97

Gloria Hunniford's
FAMILY COOKBOOK

Gloria Hunniford's FAMILY COOKBOOK

with Lena Cinnamond

SPECIAL PHOTOGRAPHY
Vernon Morgan

SUNBURST BOOKS

This edition first published in 1995 by
Sunburst Books,
Deacon House,
65 Old Church Street,
London SW3 5BS.

Acknowledgement
Photograph page 13 (top) Terry McGough

ISBN 1 85778 197 X

Publishing Manager Casey Horton

Editor Felicity Jackson

Home Economist Brigette Sargeson

Designer Ming Cheung

Photography Vernon Morgan

Stylist Fanny Ward

Printed and bound in Dublin

CONTENTS

THE HUNNIFORD FAMILY TREE

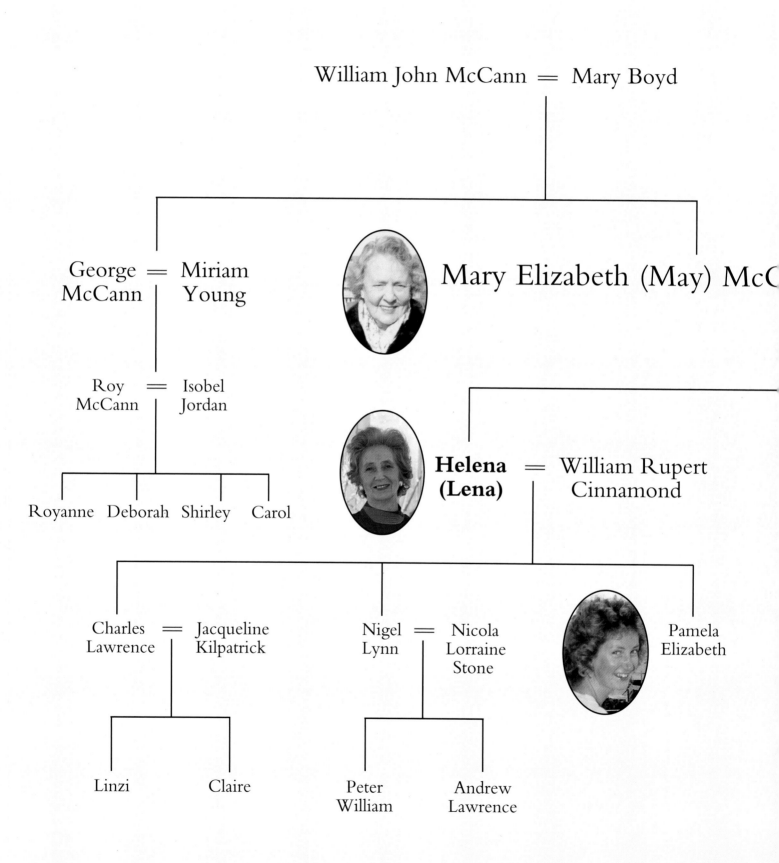

William John McCann = Mary Boyd

George = Miriam
McCann   Young

Mary Elizabeth (May) McC

Roy = Isobel
McCann   Jordan

Helena = William Rupert
(Lena)   Cinnamond

Royanne   Deborah   Shirley   Carol

Charles = Jacqueline
Lawrence   Kilpatrick

Nigel = Nicola
Lynn   Lorraine
        Stone

Pamela
Elizabeth

Linzi   Claire

Peter   Andrew
William   Lawrence

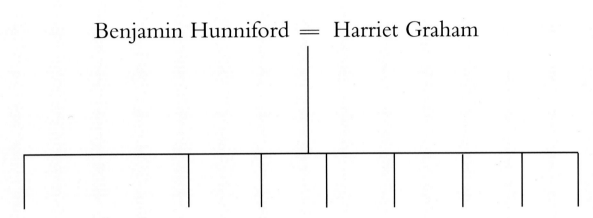

Benjamin Hunniford = Harriet Graham

= Charles Hunniford   Lillian Charlotte James Benjamin Joseph Myrtle May

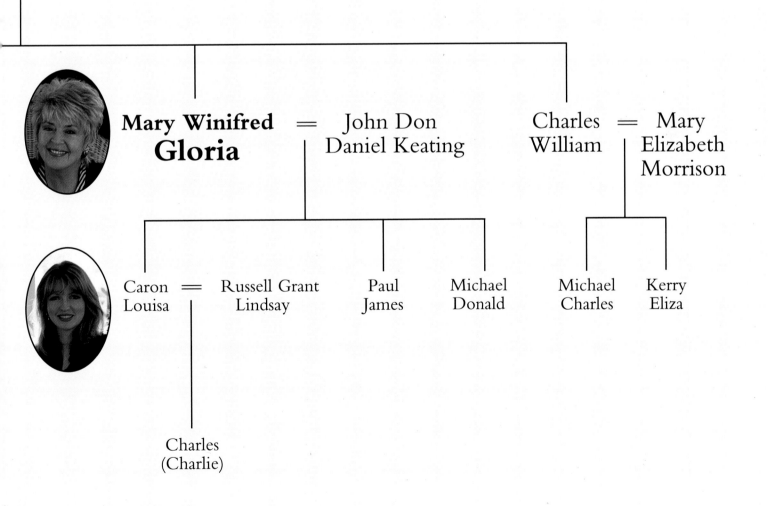

Mary Winifred
Gloria = John Don
Daniel Keating

Charles = Mary
William Elizabeth
Morrison

Caron = Russell Grant   Paul   Michael
Louisa   Lindsay   James   Donald

Michael   Kerry
Charles   Eliza

Charles
(Charlie)

Childhood Memories

'Life in Ireland revolved around food — and still does.'
GLORIA HUNNIFORD

Harriet Hunniford, Gloria's paternal grandmother, with her children. Gloria's father, Charles, is third from left.

THE HUNNIFORD FAMILY COOKBOOK began with Grandma McCann, who lived on a farm in the district of Kingarve, approximately four miles from Portadown, County Armagh, Northern Ireland. Grandma and Grandpa McCann had two children, George and May (Mary). May met and married Charles Hunniford when they were both in their teens. The Hunnifords lived with May's parents until their first child, Lena, was three years old. They then moved to their own house, 94 Armagh Road, Portadown, and this was to remain the family home for over 50 years. Following Grandpa McCann's death in 1940 when Lena was only seven years old and Gloria just a baby of three months, the children spent many weekends and school holidays on the farm with their grandma and Uncle George.

DAYS AT THE FARM

In Grandma McCann's house cooking was done over an open turf fire, as it was in many farmhouses. The kettle, griddle and pots were suspended from a small crane-like device which could be adjusted vertically or horizontally. Women judged the correct height to hang the griddle by the colour of the burning turf, or by passing their hands between griddle and flame.

Three generations: Granny McCann (back row, left), her daughter May, Gloria (front left) and Lena outside the Hunniford home in Portadown.

A studio photograph of Gloria's parents, Mary and Charles Hunniford, taken during the early days of their marriage. The couple met and married when both were in their late teens.

Charles Hunniford, semi-professional conjurer. The 'magic box' came in handy during wartime rationing; it was used to smuggle much-needed butter, sugar and flour from south of the border.

Benjamin and Harriet Hunniford in later years. Sunday supper, Ireland's 'fourth meal' of the day, was regularly taken at the Portadown home of the paternal grandparents.

August 1959: May Hunniford and Lena enjoying a well-deserved break near Newcastle.

Gloria (bottom) and childhood friend Patsy Coburn ride the hay wagon on its way from the fields back to the McCann farm.

Gloria and Lena recall their grandma baking soda farls, wheaten farls, potato farls, potato apple bread and pancakes, all on the griddle. She also baked cakes, soda bread, fruit soda bread and wheaten bread, and these were cooked in a deep cast-iron pan with a lid. This, of course, was over a good turf fire, and hot turf was placed on the lid. When the turf on the lid cooled down, it was replaced with hot turf. This process continued until the bread was baked. These breads were all so delicious that the smell of the burning turf and freshly baked bread are a vivid part of Gloria's and Lena's memories. Grandma McCann baked six days a week and perhaps that is why, to this day, fresh bread remains a favourite in both Gloria's and Lena's households.

At busy times of the year farmers sometimes hired temporary day labourers, or called on neighbours for help. One of these occasions was the hay-making season. Uncle George would have cut the grass and made hay while the sun shone. At these times Gloria and Lena loved to get to the hayfields and help turn the hay over with a pitch fork. The highlight of their day was Grandma McCann's visit to the hayfield with her large basket of food, filled with freshly-baked, warm bread oozing with butter, home-made jam and lots of hot tea.

There were orchards on the farm, their fruit trees consisting of several varieties of eating and cooking apples, pears, damsons and plums. In addition there were blackcurrant and gooseberry bushes. Uncle George also grew potatoes, garden peas and beans, and many other household vegetables.

Friends and neighbours constantly called and were made most welcome. The kettle was always on the boil, so it was a must that anyone who dropped in stayed for tea. Lena relates an amusing story about her grandfather, William John McCann, which illustrates how important food was, not only as something to feed the stomach but also as a symbol of hospitality. Grandpa McCann, when making a visit to a neighbour, was asked if he would eat an egg. Taking exception to the meanness of this offer, Grandpa McCann replied, 'I know a man who took *two* eggs the other day, and he's still alive.'

Gloria recalls with affection the importance of food and cooking in her family home in Portadown. References to the wonderful dishes which she and Lena enjoyed as children occur frequently when she talks about her childhood. Like their Grandma McCann, their mother May was a more than capable cook and was famous for her generosity and hospitality. May Hunniford baked every Saturday and

Lena and her eldest son Charles Lawrence, known as Lawrence to the family.

Caron Keating and Nigel Cinnamond in formal dress at a cousin's wedding.

Charles Hunniford celebrates his 70th birthday with his wife May, children and grandchildren.

Gloria and her three children: Michael (on Gloria's right), Caron and Paul.

Gloria and her mother celebrating home-made Irish cooking. The photograph was taken shortly before May Hunniford passed away in 1987.

frequently during the week too, so there was more than enough for everyone, including friends and all the neighbours.

SCHOOL DAYS
In the small market town of Portadown, school was near enough to home to allow the Hunniford children to ride their bikes home for lunch. As they came into the house they were greeted by the smell of a soup or stew simmering on the stove and bread and cakes baking in the oven or cooling on racks.

Gloria recalls, 'In a way, all manner of life went on around that stove. Mum was either bending over it, stirring and tasting, or sitting near it with friends or family. All you could hear then was the clicking of knitting needles and the clacking of tongues.'

At the end of the school day there was tea, and more cakes and biscuits. May Hunniford's reputation as a cook was such that her cake tins were the favourites for raiding among Lena's and Gloria's school friends.

The evening meal was not the final meal of the day. That was supper, which May Hunniford considered to be all important. No matter where anyone had been, whether they had eaten while they were out or not, they had to have supper when they came in, otherwise May would think they were ill.

'This was a proverbial banquet sometimes,' says Gloria. 'There might be a choice of savouries, including sandwiches, plus cakes, biscuits and apple tarts. We went to bed on an extremely full stomach, but, ironically, managed to stay wafer thin.'

May Hunniford always insisted on giving her children – and their children – good homemade food. When Caron was young May often looked after her during the day, and Gloria would send her off to her grandmother with a box of Caron's favourite food, tinned spaghetti. But the tins inevitably came back unopened; May Hunniford refused to have anything to do with what she called 'new-fangled fast foods'.

SUMMER FARE
The tradition of good plain cooking handed down from Grandma McCann to her daughter is kept by both Gloria and Lena, and Lena has on more than one occasion matched her mother's reputation for fine pies, cakes and breads. May Hunniford, an annual prize-winner at the premier agricultural summer fair in Portadown, usually walked away with many of the prizes, particularly for her lemon

May Hunniford's children: Gloria and Lena posed for this photograph with their brother Charles.

Above: **Caron's wedding to Russell Grant Lindsey in June 1991. Back row from the left, Paul, Gloria, Russell, Don Keating and Michael.**

Left: **Caron, Charlie and Gloria, celebrating the festive season, Christmas 1994.**

meringue pie, shortbreads and Madeira cake. But she was a modest cook, and as soon as the judges had left the marquee she would send one of the children over to see what she had won that year. Only when one of her children brought back a favourable report would she leave the house and proudly enter the tent.

BREADS AND SCONES

'Every week Mum would make nine different kinds of bread, including treacle bread, tea cake, wheaten bread and soda farls which were shaped into small triangles and fired on the griddle.'

Baking is an important part of Irish life, and Ireland boasts a wonderful variety of breads (often called cakes), baked both on and in the stove. They accompany any meal, from soda farls and potato cakes for breakfast to treacle bread at tea time, and are unique in that they use bicarbonate of soda or baking powder as the raising agent, rather than yeast.

APPLE GRIDDLE CAKE

Serves 2

225 g/8 oz cooked potato
15 g/½ oz butter or margarine
2.5 ml/½ tsp salt
30 ml/2 tbsp plain flour

For the filling:
225 g/8 oz cooking apples
sugar to taste
knob of butter

METHOD

1 Mash the potato with the butter and salt, then work in the flour. Roll the mixture to a round.
2 Peel the apples and chop them into small dice. Spread them over one half of the potato round. Sprinkle over sugar to taste and dot with the butter. Fold the other half of the potato round over the apple.
3 Heat a griddle or heavy-based frying pan. Slide the apple cake onto the griddle and cook for several minutes on each side, until lightly browned.

Variations: Double the quantity of ingredients. Roll out two potato rounds. Spread the apple over one round and place the other round on top. If preferred, omit the sugar and butter, cook the cake, then split it open across the top and add the sugar and butter through the opening.
For potato cakes, double the quantity for the potato round, roll out to a round or square, about 6mm/¼ in thick. Cut into four and cook on a griddle until browned on each side.

APPLE FRUIT LOAF

Makes 10 slices

225 g/8 oz plain flour
5 ml/1 tsp baking powder
5 ml/1 tsp bicarbonate of soda
10 ml/2 tsp ground mixed spice
100 g/4 oz butter or margarine
100 g/4 oz soft brown sugar

100 g/4 oz ready-to-eat dried apricots, chopped
100 g/4 oz sultanas
100 g/4 oz walnuts, chopped
225 g/8 oz cooking apple (peeled weight), chopped
2 eggs, beaten
milk to mix

METHOD

1 Preheat the oven to 180°C/350°F/GAS MARK 4. Grease and base line a 1.2 litre/2 pint loaf tin.
2 Sift the flour, baking powder, bicarbonate of soda and mixed spice into a bowl, and mix well. Rub the butter into the flour until the mixture resembles breadcrumbs. Stir in the sugar, apricots, sultanas, walnuts and apple, and mix well.
3 Add the beaten eggs and enough milk to make a stiff dropping consistency. Turn the mixture into the loaf tin and level the surface.
4 Bake for about 1 hour, until risen and just firm to the touch. Cool slightly in the tin, then turn out onto a wire rack to cool completely. Serve warm or cold, cut into slices, and with butter, if wished.

Variations: Use half wholemeal flour and half white flour. Substitute mashed banana for the apple. Sprinkle 15-30 ml/1-2 tbsp demerara sugar over the top of the mixture before baking.

Apple Griddle Cake

POTATO SCONES

Makes about 8-10

50 g/2 oz butter or margarine
225 g/8 oz plain flour
2.5 ml/½ tsp salt
5 ml/1 tsp baking powder

15 ml/1 tbsp sugar
50 g/2 oz mashed cooked potato
1 egg
a little milk

METHOD

1 Preheat the oven to 200°C/400°F/GAS MARK 6. Grease a baking sheet.
2 Rub the butter into the flour, then stir in the salt, baking powder, sugar and mashed potato. Mix in enough egg and milk to make a very soft dough.
3 Knead lightly, then roll out to 12 mm-1 cm/½-¾ in thick. Using a glass, pastry cutter or knife, cut out eight to ten scones.
4 Place the scones on the baking sheet and brush with egg or milk. Bake for 20-30 minutes.

OVEN SODA BREAD

Serves 4

700 g/1 ½ lb plain flour
10 ml/2 tsp sugar
7.5 ml/1 ½ tsp bicarbonate of soda

7.5 ml/1 ½ tsp cream of tartar
5 ml/1 tsp salt
450 ml/15 fl oz buttermilk

METHOD
1 Preheat the oven to 200°C/400°F/GAS MARK 6. Lightly flour a baking sheet.
2 Sift the dry ingredients together and mix in just enough buttermilk to make a fairly stiff dough.
3 Turn the dough out onto a floured surface and knead lightly until the dough has a smooth texture. Shape into a round.
4 Place on the baking sheet and cut a slash or a cross in the top.
5 Bake for 50-60 minutes. Leave to cool wrapped in a clean tea towel.

GOLDEN ROLLS

Makes 10-12

250 g/9 oz ready-made shortcrust pastry
45 ml/3 tbsp golden syrup
50-75 g/2-3 oz baked breadcrumbs
5 ml/1 tsp ground ginger
a little grated orange zest
milk or beaten egg, to glaze

METHOD

1 Preheat the oven to 400°C/200°F/GAS MARK 6.
2 On a lightly floured surface, roll out the pastry thinly and cut it into rectangles, measuring about 6-7.5 x 10 cm/2 ½-3 x 4 in.
3 Melt the golden syrup in a pan. Stir in the breadcrumbs, ginger and orange zest, and mix to form a fairly dry mixture.
4 Spread each pastry rectangle with a little of the mixture, leaving a border around the edge.
5 Roll up the pastry with the filling inside, seal both ends and crimp the end edges.Cut slits acoss the top of each roll. Place on a baking sheet, brush with milk or beaten egg and bake for 15-20 minutes.

Variation: Brush the rolls with beaten egg and sprinkle with demerara sugar before baking.

SPICED ROLLS

Makes 6-8

75 g/3 oz plain flour
40 g/1 ½ oz butter or margarine
pinch of salt
2.5 ml/½ tsp mixed spice
sugar for sprinkling

For the filling:
15 g/½ oz butter margarine
75 g/3 oz dried fruit
15 ml/1 tbsp sugar
1.25 ml/¼ tsp mixed spice
few drops of lemon juice

METHOD

1 Preheat the oven to 400°C/200°F/GAS MARK 6. Grease a baking sheet.
2 Put the flour in a bowl and rub in the butter until the mixture resembles breadcrumbs, then stir in the salt and mixed spice. Mix together well, then work in enough water to make a stiff dough.
3 To make the filling, melt the butter and stir in the fruit, sugar, mixed spice and lemon juice.
4 On a lightly floured surface, roll out the pastry to an oblong. Spread the filling on top, leaving a border around the edge. Roll up into a swiss roll shape and cut into 12 mm/½ in slices. Place them on the baking sheet and bake for 10-15 minutes. Sprinkle with sugar.

Golden Rolls

PLAIN SCONES

Makes 7

175 g/6 oz self-raising flour
pinch of salt
pinch of cream of tartar
pinch of bicarbonate of soda
50 g/2 oz butter or margarine
25g/1 oz sugar
60 ml/4 tbsp milk
beaten egg, to glaze

METHOD

1 Preheat the oven to 230°C/450°F/GAS MARK 8. Preheat a baking sheet.
2 Sift the flour, salt, cream of tartar and bicarbonate of soda into a bowl, then rub in the butter until the mixture resembles breadcrumbs. Stir in the sugar.
3 Make a well in the centre and stir in the milk to give a fairly soft dough.
4 Turn it onto a lightly floured surface, knead lightly to remove any cracks, then roll out to about 12 mm/ ½ in thick. Cut into rounds with a 5 cm/2 in cutter and place on the hot baking sheet. Brush with the beaten egg and bake for about 10 minutes, until golden brown and well risen.
5 Leave to cool on a wire rack, then serve split and buttered.

Variations: Replace half the flour with wholemeal flour. Add 50 g/2 oz mixed dried fruit, chopped glacé cherries, chopped dried apricots or chopped nuts to the dry ingredients.

GRIDDLE SCONES

Makes 24

30 ml/2 tbsp golden syrup
450 g/1 lb self-raising flour
2.5 ml/½ tsp salt
75 g/3 oz sugar
300 ml/10 fl oz milk or buttermilk
2 eggs, beaten

METHOD

1 Warm the golden syrup. Sift the flour and salt into a bowl, then stir in the sugar and warm syrup. Add the milk and beaten eggs to form a dropping consistency like thick cream.
2 Heat the griddle and lightly grease it. Drop tablespoons of mixture into rounds on the griddle, making sure they do not overlap. Turn over when little bubbles appear on the top and the bottom is golden brown, then cook on the other side.
3 Leave to cool in a clean tea towel. Serve warm or cold with butter, honey or jam.

WHEATEN BREAD

Makes 10-12 slices

225 g/8 oz plain flour
5 ml/1 tsp salt
5 ml/1 tsp bicarbonate of soda
225 g/8 oz brown flour
300 ml/10 fl oz buttermilk

METHOD

1 Preheat the oven to 230°C/450°F/GAS MARK 8. Lightly flour a baking sheet.
2 Sift the plain flour, salt and bicarbonate of soda into a bowl and stir in the brown flour. Mix together, then stir in the buttermilk.
3 Turn out onto a floured surface and knead lightly. Shape the dough into a round.
4 Place the loaf on the lightly floured baking sheet and bake for about 1 hour. Leave to cool wrapped in a tea towel.

Note: This bread can also be baked in a 900 g/2 lb loaf tin dusted with flour.

TREACLE SCONES

Makes 7

175 g/6 oz plain flour
pinch of salt
5 ml/1 tsp bicarbonate of soda
2.5 ml/1/2 tsp ground mixed spice
25 g/1 oz butter or margarine
15 ml/1 tbsp soft brown sugar
15 ml/1 tbsp treacle
100 ml/4 fl oz buttermilk
beaten egg, to glaze

METHOD

1 Preheat the oven to 230°C/450°F/GAS MARK 8. Preheat a baking sheet.
2 Sift the flour, salt, bicarbonate of soda and mixed spice into a bowl, then rub in the butter until the mixture resembles breadcrumbs. Stir in the sugar.
3 Add the treacle and buttermilk and mix to a fairly soft dough. Turn onto a lightly floured surface, knead lightly to remove any cracks, then roll out to about 12 mm/½ in thick. Cut the dough into rounds with a 5 cm/2 in cutter and place on the hot baking sheet. Brush with the beaten egg and bake for about 10 minutes, until golden and well risen.
4 Leave to cool on a wire rack, then serve warm or cold, split and buttered.

Variation: For a richer scone mixture, rub in 40 g/1 ½ oz butter and add an egg.

TREACLE BREAD

Makes approximately 12 slices

30-45 ml/2-3 tbsp black treacle
200 ml/7 fl oz buttermilk
400 g/14 oz plain flour
2.5 ml/½ tsp salt
2.5 ml/½ tsp ground ginger
2.5 ml/½ tsp mixed spice
5 ml/1 tsp bicarbonate of soda
75 g/3 oz caster sugar
75 g/3 oz margarine

METHOD

1 Preheat the oven to 180°C/350°F/GAS MARK 4. Grease and flour a 20 cm/8 in square cake tin.
2 Melt the treacle and mix with the buttermilk.
3 Sift the dry ingredients together and rub in the margarine.
4 Pour in the treacle and buttermilk and mix to a soft consistency.
5 Turn in to the cake tin and bake for about 1 hour, until golden and cooked through. Cover with foil during cooking, if necessary, to prevent overbrowning.

Note: If you like a strong black treacle flavour, use 45 ml/3 tbsp; if you prefer a milder taste, use 30 ml/2 tbsp.

TEA CAKE

Makes about 12 slices

350 g/12 oz self-raising flour
pinch of salt
100 g/4 oz sugar
100 g/4 oz butter or margarine
100 g/4 oz sultanas (optional)
1 egg, beaten
90 ml/6 tbsp milk

METHOD

1 Preheat the oven to 180°C/350°F/GAS MARK 4. Grease and flour a 20 cm/8 in square tin.
2 Sift the flour and salt into a bowl. Add the sugar and rub in the butter. Stir in the sultanas, if using.
3 Add the beaten egg and milk, and mix to a soft consistency.
4 Turn in to the sandwich tin and bake for 30 minutes. Eat the day it is made, spread with butter.

Variation: Add 2.5 ml/½ tsp ground cinnamon or a little grated lemon or orange zest.

Treacle Bread

SODA FARLS

Makes 4

450 g/1 lb plain flour
10 ml/2 tsp sugar
5 ml/1 tsp bicarbonate of soda
5 ml/1 tsp cream of tartar
2.5 ml/½ tsp salt
300 ml/10 fl oz buttermilk

METHOD

1 Sift the dry ingredients into a bowl, make a well in the centre and mix in half the buttermilk. Using a knife, draw in the flour from the sides of the bowl, adding more buttermilk as the batter thickens. The mixing should be done with as little working as possible until the mixture leaves the sides of the bowl fairly cleanly.
2 Turn out onto a floured surface and knead lightly, turning the corners into the centre and turning the round as you do so. When smooth underneath, turn it upside down .
3 Lightly roll out to a round 12 mm/½ in thick. Cut into four quarters (farls).
4 Heat a griddle over low heat (see Note). Place the farls on the griddle and cook for 5-6 minutes, until they have risen and there is a white skin on top.
5 Increase the heat and continue cooking until the farls are brown on the bottom. Turn them over and cook on the other side -- it takes about 15 minutes from the time the farls are put on the griddle.

Note: The griddle should be just hot enough to prevent the farls sticking: if a sprinkling of flour browns when it is thrown on the griddle, it is too hot.

Variation: Add finely chopped herbs to the mixture. Serve the farls with cheese.

POTATO AND OAT FARLS

Makes 4

6 medium-sized potatoes, cooked
5 ml/1 tsp salt
knob of butter
oatmeal

METHOD

1 Mash the potatoes and stir in the salt and butter. Work in enough oatmeal to form a soft dough.
2 Turn onto a surface scattered with oatmeal and form into a round or square. Cut into quarters (farls) or squares.
3 Heat a griddle. Cook the farls on the hot griddle until browned on both sides. Eat hot or cold with plenty of butter.

Variation: These farls are very good served with bacon. If preferred, cook the bacon and keep it warm while frying the farls in the bacon fat.

Soda Farls

SOUPS AND STARTERS

'A cast-iron, crane-like contraption swung over the flames of Granny McCann's kitchen fireplace, and from it hung this huge black cauldron bubbling with soup for the family.'

Irish soups provide a warming, satisfying starter, or may make a meal in themselves. Potatoes, probably Ireland's most traditional food, are used in many dishes, including the delicious soup in this chapter. Other family starters include savoury pastries, such as individual tomato and basil tarts and cheesy celery rolls.

CREAM OF POTATO SOUP

Serves 4-6

50 g/2 oz butter
2 onions, sliced
1 leek, sliced
900 g/2 lb potatoes, diced
900 ml/1 ½ pints vegetable or chicken stock

salt and pepper
450 ml/15 fl oz milk
150 ml/5 fl oz single cream
chopped fresh chives, to garnish

METHOD

1 Melt the butter in a large pan and gently fry the onions, leek and potatoes for 5 minutes, stirring frequently.
2 Stir in the stock and season with salt and pepper. Cover and simmer gently for 40 minutes.
3 Cool slightly, then purée in a blender or food processor. Return the soup to the pan.
4 Add the milk and reheat. Taste and adjust the seasoning. Serve hot with swirls of cream and garnished with the chives.

Note: This soup is good served with garlic-flavoured croûtons.

MUSSEL AND HERBED TOMATO SOUP

Serves 4

900 g/ 2 lb mussels in their shells
60 ml/4 tbsp vegetable oil
1 large onion, chopped
1-2 garlic cloves, crushed
400 g/14 oz can chopped tomatoes
1 litre/1 ¾ pints chicken stock
225 ml/8 fl oz dry white wine
45 ml/3 tbsp tomato purée

30 ml/2 tbsp shredded fresh basil leaves
15 ml/1 tbsp chopped fresh parsley
2 pinches of dried thyme
15-30 ml/1-2 tbsp shredded celery leaves
salt and pepper
60 ml/4 tbsp double cream
shredded basil leaves, to garnish

METHOD

1 Scrub the mussels and remove the beards. Discard any damaged mussels and any that are open and do not close when sharply tapped with the back of a knife.
2 Heat the oil in a pan and gently fry the onion and garlic for 5 minutes. Add the tomatoes, chicken stock, 150 ml/5 fl oz of the wine, the tomato purée, herbs, celery leaves and salt and pepper. Cover and simmer gently for 15 minutes.
3 Place the mussels in a large pan with the remaining wine and 75 ml/3 fl oz water. Cover and bring to the boil. Reduce the heat and cook for 3-4 minutes, shaking the pan frequently until the mussels open. Remove from the heat, drain the mussels, reserving the cooking liquid. Discard any mussels that have not opened.
4 Add 150 ml/5 fl oz of the mussel cooking liquid to the tomato mixture. Taste and adjust the seasoning, if necessary.
5 Spoon the soup into four warmed soup bowls. Lightly stir 1 tbsp cream into each one to marble it. Add the mussels and sprinkle shredded basil leaves over the top. Serve hot.

Cream of Potato Soup
Mussel and Herbed Tomato Soup

COTTAGE SOUP

Serves 4

25 g/1 oz butter or margarine
225 g/8 oz potatoes, diced
225 g/8 oz carrots, diced
2 leeks or onions, sliced
1 or 2 sticks celery, finely chopped
900 ml/1 ½ pints stock or water
salt and pepper
25 g/1 oz plain flour
300 ml/10 fl oz milk
50 g/2 oz Cheddar cheese, grated

METHOD

1 Melt the butter in a pan and fry all the vegetables until the fat has been absorbed. Add the stock and season with salt and pepper. Bring to the boil and simmer for about 45 minutes.
2 Blend the flour with the milk and stir it into the soup. Bring back to the boil and boil for 2-3 minutes.
3 Pour the soup into individual bowls and sprinkle the cheese over the top.

TOMATO SOUP

Serves 4

50 g/2 oz ham or bacon (you can use trimmings), cut into small pieces
1 onion, chopped
450 g/1 lb tomatoes, cut into quarters
900 ml/1 ½ pints stock
salt and pepper
25 g/1 oz butter or margarine
40 g/1 ½ oz plain flour
150 ml/5 fl oz milk
5 ml/1 tsp sugar

METHOD

1 Place the bacon and onion in a pan and sauté over low heat for about 15 minutes.
2 Add the tomatoes, stock and salt and pepper. Bring to the boil and simmer until the vegetables are tender. Rub the mixture through a sieve or purée in a blender or food processor.
3 Melt the butter in the soup pan, add the flour and cook for 1 minute. Gradually stir in the milk. Add the purée and sugar. Bring to the boil and boil for 2-3 minutes.
4 Serve the soup with toast or fried bread.

CAULIFLOWER SOUP

Serves 4

1 cauliflower, divided into florets
salt and pepper
20 g/¾ oz butter or margarine
20 g/¾ oz plain flour

450 ml/15 fl oz vegetable stock
300 ml/10 fl oz milk
5 ml/1 tsp sugar

METHOD

1 Cook the cauliflower in boiling salted water for 10 minutes. Drain the cauliflower and reserve a few florets for garnishing.
2 Bring the vegetable stock to the boil, add the rest of the cauliflower and continue cooking until it is tender. Purée in a blender or food processor or rub through a sieve.
3 Melt the butter in the soup pan, add the flour and cook for 1 minute. Gradually stir in the milk. Add the purée and sugar. Bring to the boil and boil for 2 minutes.
4 Season with salt and pepper and stir in the reserved cauliflower florets.

VEGETABLE SOUP

Serves 4

100 g/4 oz soup mix (barley, peas, lentils)
1 large marrow or ham bone
50 g/2 oz butter
2 sticks celery
225 g/8 oz carrots, sliced
225 g/8 oz swede or turnips, diced

225 g/8 oz potatoes, diced
1 large onion, chopped
2 leeks, shredded
2 beef or vegetable stock cubes
salt and pepper
30 ml/2 tbsp chopped fresh parsley

METHOD

1 Soak the soup mix overnight in enough cold water to cover.
2 The next day, drain the soup mix and place in a large pan with 1.2 litres/2 pints water. Bring to the boil and boil rapidly for 10 minutes. Add the marrow bone, partly cover the pan and simmer gently for 1 hour.
3 Meanwhile, melt the butter in a separate pan, add the prepared vegetables and sauté gently for 5 minutes. Add the stock cubes and 1.2 litres/2 pints water, bring to the boil, then add to the pan containing the soup mix. Simmer gently for 1 hour, stirring occasionally.
4 Taste and adjust the seasoning, if necessary. Remove the marrow bone and stir in the parsley. Serve hot, garnished with the celery leaves.

Note: This soup tastes best if it is made ahead and then left to stand for several hours before reheating. It is an easy recipe to double up if cooking for a large number of people.

SMOKED HADDOCK PATE

Serves 4

350 g/12 oz smoked haddock
50 g/2 oz butter
150 ml/5 fl oz double cream
30 ml/2 tbsp lemon juice
5 ml/1 tsp Worcestershire sauce
black pepper
lemon slices and chopped fresh herbs, to garnish

METHOD

1 Place the fish in a shallow pan and cover with boiling water. Cover and simmer for 10 minutes. Drain the fish, then remove the skin and flake the fish.
2 Melt the butter, pour it over the fish and mix well. Mash the fish, then rub it through a sieve, or purée in a blender or food processor.
3 Whip the cream until it is fluffy. Fold in the fish, then add the lemon juice and Worcestershire sauce. Season to taste with black pepper.
4 Pour the mixture into a large round serving dish and chill in the refrigerator. Serve garnished with slices of lemon and chopped herbs.

CHEESY CELERY ROLLS

Makes 10-12

For the rough puff pastry:
225 g/8 oz plain flour
pinch of salt
75 g/3 oz butter or block margarine, well chilled
75 g/3 oz lard
about 150 ml/5 fl oz chilled water
squeeze of lemon juice

For the filling:
100 g/4 oz Cheddar cheese, grated
2 sticks celery, chopped
1 small onion, chopped
100 g/4 oz potatoes, grated
175 g/6 oz mushrooms, finely chopped
15 ml/1 tbsp chopped fresh mixed herbs
salt and pepper

METHOD

1 To make the pastry, mix the flour and salt together. Cut the butter into 2 cm/¾ in cubes and stir it into the flour without breaking it up. Add enough water and lemon juice to make a fairly stiff dough.
2 On a lightly floured surface, roll out the pastry to an oblong three times as long as it is wide. Fold the bottom third up and the top third down. Turn the pastry so the folded edges are at the sides and seal the ends with a rolling pin. Wrap and chill for 15 minutes.

3 Repeat the rolling and folding process three more times. Wrap and chill for 30 minutes.

4 Preheat the oven to 220°C/425°F/GAS MARK 7. Grease a baking sheet.

5 To make the filling, mix the cheese with the celery, onion, potatoes, mushrooms and herbs, and season with salt and pepper.

6 Roll out the pastry to an oblong, then cut in half lengthwise to make two strips. Place half the filling down the centre of each strip.

7 Dampen the edges and fold over, pressing them together. Flake with a knife and cut the pastry into rolls 40-50 cm/1 ½-2 in long. Slash the tops to allow steam to escape.

8 Place on the baking sheet and bake for 25-30 minutes, until golden brown. Serve with salad leaves.

Sausage Rolls

Makes 12

For the flaky pastry:
225 g/8 oz plain flour
pinch of salt
175 g/6 oz butter or half and half butter and lard, softened
120 ml/8 tbsp chilled water
squeeze of lemon juice
1 egg, beaten

For the filling:
225 g/8 oz sausagemeat
10 ml/2 tsp dried sage

METHOD

1 To make the pastry, mix the flour and salt. Divide the butter into quarters. Add one quarter to the flour and rub in. Add enough water and lemon juice to make an elastic dough.

2 On a lightly floured surface, roll out the pastry to an oblong three times as long as it is wide. Dot another portion of butter over the top two thirds of the pastry. Fold bottom of pastry up and top third down.

3 Turn the pastry so folded edges are at the sides. Seal the edges with a rolling pin. Wrap and seal for 15 minutes.

4 Re-roll and repeat the process twice more. Wrap and chill for 30 minutes.

5 Preheat the oven to 200°C/400°F/GAS MARK 6. To make the filling, mix the sausagemeat and sage. On a floured surface, form the filling into two rolls.

6 Roll out the pastry to an oblong, then cut in half lengthwise to make two strips. Place a sausagemeat roll on each strip of pastry. Dampen the pastry edges and form it into a roll. Cut each roll into six slices. Brush with beaten egg and bake for 30 minutes. Serve with crusty bread and a side salad.

Variation: For a more flavoursome filling, use sausages with added herbs or spices instead of sausagemeat. Skin the sausages and then use in the same way as the sausagemeat.

TOMATO AND BASIL TARTS

Serves 6

250 g/9 oz ready-made shortcrust pastry
700 g/1 ½ lb tomatoes
1 small onion, finely chopped
30 ml/2 tbsp chopped fresh basil

2 eggs, beaten
100 g/4 oz fresh breadcrumbs
100 g/4 oz Cheddar cheese
salt and pepper

METHOD

1 Preheat the oven to 200°C/400F/GAS MARK 6.
2 On a lightly floured surface, roll out the pastry and use to line six individual tartlet tins. Chill the pastry in the refrigerator for 10-15 minutes, then bake blind for 5 minutes. Reduce the oven temperature to 180°C/350°F/GAS MARK 4.
3 Skin and finely chop the tomatoes. Place in a bowl and mix in the onion, basil, eggs, half the breadcrumbs and half the cheese. Season with salt and pepper.
4 Pour the mixture into the pastry case. Mix together the remaining breadcrumbs and cheese and sprinkle the mixture over the filling. Bake for 15-20 minutes, until cooked and golden brown. Serve with mixed salad leaves.

Variations: Instead of individual tarts, make one large flan using a deep 23 cm/9 in round flan tin. Bake blind for 10 minutes, then bake the filled flan for 30 minutes. The flan could be served as a main course with a jacket potatoes and steamed vegetables or a mixed salad.
Substitute other cheeses, such as Stilton, Cheshire or Double Gloucester, for the Cheddar, if preferred.

BEETROOT AND PRUNE SALAD

Serves 4

1 lettuce or mixed lettuce leaves
40-50 g/1 ½-2 oz soft cheese
10-15 ml/2-3 tsp chutney
8-12 large cooked prunes, stoned

2 cooked beetroot
30-45 ml/2-3 tbsp chopped fresh herbs
French dressing

METHOD

1 Tear the lettuce into bite-sized pieces and arrange on individual serving plates.
2 Mix the cheese and chutney together and spoon the mixture into the stoned prunes.
3 Dice the beetroot and arrange on the lettuce leaves. Place the prunes on top and scatter with fresh herbs. Drizzle a little dressing over the top and serve at once.

Note: In summer, this salad can be decorated with edible flowers, such as nasturtiums.

Variation: The prunes can be filled with grated cheese, such as Cheddar, if preferred.

Tomato and Basil Tarts

MAIN
COURSES

'I'd pedal home from school for lunch to be met by the aroma of home-made stew made with potatoes and carrots from the garden.'

Irish meals are basically hearty and wholesome, using fresh local ingredients – home-reared lamb, fish from the rivers and sea, rich farmhouse butter, and potatoes and apples – all cooked simply, without the need for rich sauces or elaborate flavourings.

STEAK DIANE

Serves 4

700 g/1 ½ lb sirloin or rump steak,
*   trimmed of excess fat and cut into 4 pieces*
mustard powder
about 50 g/2 oz butter
garlic salt and pepper

1 large onion, finely sliced
350 g/12 oz mushrooms, chopped
30 ml/2 tbsp brandy
150 ml/5 fl oz double cream
Worcestershire sauce

METHOD

1 Flatten the steaks slightly and coat it in mustard powder. Melt 50 g/2 oz butter in a frying pan and fry the steaks (see Note), adding garlic salt and pepper to taste. When cooked, remove the steaks and keep warm.

2 Add the sliced onion and mushrooms to the pan, adding a little more butter if necessary, and cook for 3-5 minutes, until the onion is cooked. Stir in the Worcestershire sauce, brandy and cream, and season with garlic salt and pepper. Stir until well mixed, then pour the sauce over the steaks and serve immediately, accompanied by salad leaves.

Note: Cook 2 cm/¾ in steaks for 2 ½ minutes each side for rare, 4 minutes each side for medium, and about 6 minutes each side for well done. Take care not to overcook them.

ROAST STUFFED STEAK

Serves 4

450 g/1 lb lean braising steak (in a thick slice)
45 ml/3 tbsp vegetable oil or dripping
1-2 leeks, cut into large pieces
2 onions, quartered, or 8 whole shallots

175 g/6 oz swede, cut into pieces
1 parsnip, quartered
2 large carrots, quartered
600 ml/1 pint beef stock or water

For the stuffing:

25 g/1 oz butter
1 onion, chopped
50 g/2 oz fresh breadcrumbs
1 garlic clove, crushed (optional)

1 egg, beaten
30 ml/2 tbsp chopped fresh parsley
*   or herb of your choice*
salt and pepper

METHOD

1 Preheat the oven to 180°C/350°F/GAS MARK 4.

2 To make the stuffing, melt the butter in a pan and fry the onion and garlic for 3 minutes. Remove from the heat and stir in the breadcrumbs, beaten egg, herbs and salt and pepper. Mix well.

3 Using a sharp knife, cut a neat pocket in the steak and fill with the prepared stuffing. Secure in a neat shape with wooden cocktail sticks, or tie with fine string.

4 Heat the oil or dripping in a flameproof casserole and fry the steak on each side until seared and coloured, about 5 minutes. Remove the meat from the casserole. Add the leeks, onions, swede, parsnip and carrots to the casserole and fry for a few minutes. Stir in the stock or water and bring to the boil. Remove from the heat gnd place the steak on top of the vegetables. Season with salt and pepper.

5 Cover and cook for about 1 ½ hours, or until the meat is tender, basting it occasionally with stock. Remove the cocktail sticks or string and serve the meat cut into slices, accompanied by the vegetables and cooking liquid, thickened if wished.

Steak Diane

BEEF AND POTATO BAKE

Serves 4

700 g/1 ½ lb potatoes, cooked and mashed
 40 g/1½ oz butter
1 ½ eggs, beaten

40 g/1 ½ oz Cheddar cheese, finely grated
freshly grated nutmeg
salt and pepper

For the filling:

45 ml/3 tbsp vegetable oil
350 g/12 oz minced beef
1 onion, chopped
2 sticks celery, thinly sliced
100 g/4 oz mushrooms, sliced

½ red pepper, cored and diced
½ green pepper, cored and diced
225 g/8 oz tomatoes, chopped
150 ml/5 fl oz beef stock
chopped flat-leaf parsley, to garnish

METHOD

1 Preheat the oven to 200°C/400°F/GAS MARK 6. Add the butter, eggs and cheese to the potato and season to taste with nutmeg, salt and pepper. Beat until smooth. Transfer to a large piping bag fitted with a large star nozzle and pipe a border of potato into an ovenproof dish. Bake for 20-25 minutes.

2 Meanwhile, heat the oil in a pan and gently fry the minced beef, onion, celery, mushrooms and peppers for 5 minutes, stirring to break up the meat. Stir in the tomatoes, breaking them up, then add the stock. Season with salt and pepper. Cook gently for 20 minutes, or until the meat is cooked, stirring frequently.

3 Spoon the mixture into the centre of the potato border and serve hot, garnished with chopped parsley.

SAVOURY MEAT AND VEGETABLE DUMPLING

Serves 4

For the suet pastry:

225 g/8 oz self-raising flour
good pinch of salt
100 g/4 oz shredded suet

For the filling:

225-350 g/8-12 oz braising steak, diced
30 ml/2 tbsp seasoned flour
2 carrots, thinly sliced
100 g/4 oz swede or turnip, diced

1 ½ leeks, halved and sliced
15-30 ml/1-2 tbsp chopped fresh
* or 1 tsp dried mixed herbs*
300 ml/10 fl oz cold beef stock or water

METHOD

1 Grease a 1.2 litre/2 pint pudding basin. To make the pastry, mix together the flour, salt and suet in a bowl. Add enough cold water to form a fairly soft dough. Reserve one third of the dough for the lid. Roll out the rest and use to line the pudding basin. Toss the steak in the seasoned flour. Layer the meat and vegetables in the basin. Sprinkle in the herbs and any remaining flour. Pour in the stock.

2 Roll out the remaining pastry to make a lid. Dampen the edges and place in position. Press the edges well to seal them. Cover the pudding with greased greaseproof paper with a centre fold to allow for expansion. Tie with string. Steam the pudding for 3 ½ -4 hours, topping up the pan with boiling water, as necessary.

BAKED BEEF STEAK PUDDING

Serves 4-6

700 g/1 ½ lb stewing steak, cut into cubes
225 g/8 oz kidney, cubed
1 onion, sliced
300 ml/10 fl oz beef stock
salt and pepper
175 g/6 oz plain flour
2 eggs, beaten
450 ml/15 fl oz milk
30 ml/2 tbsp vegetable oil

METHOD

1 Place the beef, kidney, onion and stock in a pan. Bring to the boil, reduce the heat and simmer, covered, for 1 ½-2 hours, until the meat is tender.
2 Preheat the oven to 220°C/425°F/GAS MARK 7. Strain the meat (use the stock for other recipes) and season with salt and pepper.
3 Sift the flour and a pinch of salt into a bowl. Beat in the eggs and milk to make a smooth batter.
4 Heat the oil in a small roasting tin, about 28 x 20 cm/11 x 8 in, for about 5 minutes, until hot. Spread the meat mixture in the tin and pour the batter over it.
5 Bake for 30-45 minutes, until risen and golden brown.

SAVOURY MEAT BALLS

Serves 4

700 g/1 ½ lb lean minced beef
2 onions, finely chopped
salt and pepper
pinch of paprika
1 egg, beaten
garlic salt
two 295 g/10 oz cans condensed cream of tomato soup

METHOD

1 Preheat the oven to 180°C/350°F/GAS MARK 4. Grease a casserole or an ovenproof dish with a lid.
2 Put the minced beef, onions, salt, pepper and paprika in a bowl, add the beaten egg and mix well.
3 Form the meat mixture into balls and arrange them in the dish. Sprinkle with pepper and garlic salt.
4 Pour the soup over the top. Cover the dish and cook for about 1 ½ hours. Serve with creamy mashed potatoes and a green vegetable.

TRIPE AND LENTILS

Serves 4

450 g/1 lb dressed tripe
1 onion, chopped
175 g/6 oz mushrooms, sliced
100 g/4 oz whole green lentils
1 bay leaf (optional)

salt and pepper
600 ml/1 pint milk
30 ml/2 tbsp cornflour
15 ml/1 tbsp chopped fresh parsley

METHOD

1 Cut the tripe into small pieces. Place it in a pan and add the onion, mushrooms, lentils and bay leaf. Season with salt and pepper, then pour in the milk.
2 Bring to the boil, cover and simmer gently for 2 hours, until tender.
3 Mix the cornflour with a little water and stir it into the pan. Cook for 2 minutes.
4 Stir in the parsley and serve at once, with fingers of toast or mashed potato.

MEAT AND VEGETABLE PIE

Serves 4

175 g/6 oz ready-made shortcrust pastry
milk, to glaze

For the filling:

45 ml/3 tbsp vegetable oil or dripping
225 g/8 oz braising steak,
    cut into thin strips
1 onion, chopped
1 potato, diced
100 g/4 oz swede, diced
1 large carrot, sliced

75 g/3 oz parsnip, diced
1 stick celery, sliced
30 ml/2 tbsp plain flour
15 ml/1 tbsp tomato purée
450 ml/15 fl oz beef stock
dash of Worcestershire sauce
salt and pepper

METHOD

1 To make the filling, heat the oil or dripping in a pan and fry the meat and vegetables for 5 minutes, stirring frequently.
2 Stir in the flour and cook for 1 minute. Stir in the tomato purée and stock, and season with Worcestershire sauce and salt and pepper. Mix well, then cover and cook gently for 1-1 ¼ hours, stirring frequently, until tender and cooked through. Leave to cool.
3 Preheat the oven to 190°C/375°F/GAS MARK 5. On a lightly floured surface, roll out the pastry 5 cm/2 in wider than a 900 ml-1.2 litre/1 ½-2 pint pie dish. Cut a 2.5 cm/1 in wide strip from the outer edge. Dampen the rim of the dish and place the pastry strip on it.
4 Spoon the meat and vegetable mixture into the dish. Lift the remaining pastry on the rolling pin and lay it over the pie dish. Press the lid lightly on to the rim to seal. Scallop the edges, if wished. Roll out the pastry trimmings and use to decorate the pie. Brush with beaten egg and cut a slit in the centre to allow the steam to escape. Bake for 45 minutes, until golden brown. Serve hot or cold.

STEAK AND MUSHROOM CASSEROLE

Serves 4

30 ml/2 tbsp vegetable oil
700 g/1 ½ lb lean stewing steak,
  cut into cubes
225 g/8 oz baby onion
25 g/1 oz plain flour
150 ml/5 fl oz beef stock
300 ml/10 fl oz red wine

225 g/8 oz carrots, sliced
225 g/8 oz button mushrooms
5 ml/1 tsp dried thyme
salt and pepper
450 g/1 lb creamed potatoes
chopped fresh parsley, to garnish

METHOD

1 Preheat the oven to 170°C/325°F/GAS MARK 3.
2 Heat the oil in a flameproof casserole, add the meat and brown on all sides. Remove from the casserole with a slotted spoon.
3 Add the onions to the casserole and fry gently until translucent.
4 Add the flour and cook briefly, then remove from the heat and stir in the stock and the wine. Add the mushrooms, carrots and thyme. Bring to the boil.
5 Return the meat to the casserole and season with salt and pepper. Cover and cook in the oven for 2 ½ hours, until the meat is tender.
6 Pipe a border of creamed potato around the top of the casserole and serve garnished with chopped parsley. Serve with steamed runner or green beans, sprouts or mashed swede.

Variations: Use whole baby carrots instead of sliced carrots. Add 100 g/4 oz diced smoked back bacon and 1 crushed clove of garlic for extra flavour.

OXTAIL CASSEROLE

Serves 4

15 ml/1 tbsp vegetable oil
1 oxtail, trimmed and cut into pieces
1 onion, sliced
400 g/14 oz can chopped tomatoes
4 cloves

1 bay leaf
salt and pepper
350 g/12 oz parsnips, diced
30 ml/2 tbsp cornflour

METHOD

1 Heat the oil in a flameproof casserole, add the oxtail pieces and brown on all sides. Remove from the casserole with a slotted spoon.
2 Add the onions to the casserole and cook gently until translucent.
3 Add the tomatoes, stock, cloves and bay leaf, and season with salt and pepper.
4 Cover and bring to the boil, then reduce the heat and simmer very slowly for 2 hours.
5 Skim off the fat. Add the diced parsnip, re-cover and cook for a further 1 hour.
6 Mix the cornflour with a little cold water, then stir it into the casserole and cook for 2-3 minutes. Serve with new or jacket potatoes and green vegetables, such as broccoli, beans or courgettes.

Variations: Use red wine instead of the stock. Substitute swede or turnip in place of the parsnip. Add chopped fresh herbs instead the bay leaf.

Oxtail Casserole
Steak and Mushroom Casserole

IRISH STEW

Serves 4-6

900 g/2 lb potatoes, thinly sliced
900 g/2 lb best end of neck lamb chops
450 g/1 lb onions, thinly sliced
4 carrots, thinly sliced
2 parsnips, halved and thinly sliced

salt and pepper
15 ml/1 tbsp chopped fresh parsley
15 ml/1 tbsp chopped fresh thyme
25 g/1 oz butter
thyme sprigs, to garnish

METHOD

1 Preheat the oven to 190°C/3375°F/GAS MARK 5.

2 Arrange one third of the sliced potatoes in a casserole and add half the chops, onions, carrots and parsnips. Season well with salt and pepper and sprinkle with half the chopped herbs.

3 Repeat these layers once more and finish with a layer of potatoes. Pour over 600 ml/1 pint water, cover with buttered greaseproof paper (using a little of the butter) and a lid.

4 Bake for 1 ½ hours, then remove the lid and the greaseproof paper. Dot the potatoes with the remaining butter and cook, uncovered, for a further 10-15 minutes. Garnish with thyme sprigs and serve hot with soda bread.

Note: While an authentic Irish stew is made with just lamb, potatoes and onions, the extra vegetables in this version give added colour. For a juicier stew, add 750 ml/1 ¼ pints water instead of 600 ml/1 pint.

CHAMP

Serves 6

1.8 kg/4 lb potatoes (new floury
   ones are best), halved
salt and pepper
75 g/3 oz butter

approximately 175 ml/6 fl oz milk
6 spring onions, finely chopped
chopped chives, to garnish

METHOD

1 Cook the potatoes in boiling salted water until tender. Drain well, then put them back on a very low heat, covering the pan with a clean tea towel, to dry out the potatoes.

2 When dry, mash the potatoes with some of the butter.

3 Put the milk in a pan with the spring onions and bring to the boil. Pour the mixture onto the mashed potato and mix in. Do not make the potato too sloppy: if this does happen, dry it out a little over low heat.

4 Spoon the potato into individual bowls, make a small well in the centre and add the remaining butter. Serve garnished with chopped chives.

Note: This buttery potato dish makes a tasty accompaniment to serve with hearty casseroles, joints of meat or fish dishes.

Irish Stew

LIVER AND ONIONS

Serves 4

40 g/1 ½ oz butter
2 large onions, sliced
50 g/2 oz fresh breadcrumbs
pinch of dried thyme or sage

salt and pepper
450 g/1 lb lamb's liver, thinly sliced
100 g/4 oz mushrooms, sliced
225 ml/8 fl oz stock

METHOD

1 Preheat the oven to 180°C/350°F/GAS MARK 4.
2 Melt 25 g/1 oz of the butter in a frying pan and fry the onions until softened. In a separate pan, melt the remaining butter, then stir in the breadcrumbs and thyme or sage. Season with salt and pepper.
3 Spread the breadcrumb mixture in the bottom of an ovenproof dish. Arrange the liver slices on top, cover with the mushrooms, then top with the onions. Pour the stock over the top, cover and cook for 1 hour.

LAMB AND ONION PIE

Serves 4

250 g/9 oz ready-made shortcrust pastry
beaten egg, to glaze

For the filling:

15 ml/1 tbsp vegetable oil
450 g/1 lb lamb fillet, cubed
1 onion, sliced
1 garlic clove, crushed
1 large leek, sliced
2 carrots, sliced

1 large cooking apple, peeled and chopped
450 g/1 lb potatoes, thinly sliced
150 ml/5 fl oz stock
10 ml/2 tsp dried mixed herbs
salt and pepper

METHOD

1 Preheat the oven to 220°C/425°F/GAS MARK 7. Grease an ovenproof dish.
2 To make the filling, heat the oil in a pan and brown the lamb cubes on all sides. Remove with a slotted spoon and keep warm.
3 Add the onion, garlic, leek and carrots and sauté for 3 minutes. Add the apple and cook for 1 minute. Return the meat to the pan and mix well.
4 Place half the potato slices in the base of the dish and cover with half the meat mixture. Repeat the layers. Mix the stock, herbs and salt and pepper, and pour it over the meat.
5 On a lightly floured surface, roll out the pastry 5 cm/2 in wider than the dish. Cut a 2.5 cm/1 in wide strip from the outer edge. Dampen the rim of the dish and place the pastry strip on it. Lift the remaining pastry on the rolling pin and lay it over the pie dish. Press lid lightly on the rim to seal. Scallop or flute the edges, if wished. Roll out the pastry trimmings and use to decorate the pie. Brush with the beaten egg and cut a slit in the centre to allow the steam to escape.
6 Bake for 15 minutes, then reduce the oven temperature to 180°C/350°F/GAS MARK 4 and cook for a further 45 minutes.

Lamb and Onion Pie

STUFFED PORK FILLET

Serves 4

3 pork fillets (tenderloins)
100 g/4 oz thin rashers streaky bacon, rinded

150 ml/5 fl oz white wine
15 ml/1 tbsp vegetable oil

For the stuffing:

15 ml/1 tbsp vegetable oil
1 onion, chopped
1-2 sticks celery, finely chopped
50 g/2 oz back bacon, rinded and finely chopped
75 g/3 oz fresh breadcrumbs

225 g/8 oz cooking apple, peeled and grated or chopped
5 ml/1 tsp dried sage
15 ml/1 tbsp chopped fresh parsley
salt and pepper
1 egg, beaten

METHOD

1 Preheat the oven to 180°C/350°F/GAS MARK 4.
2 To make the stuffing, heat the oil in a pan and fry the onion, celery and back bacon for 5 minutes. Add the breadcrumbs, apple, sage, parsley, salt and pepper, and enough egg to combine the mixture.
3 Slit the fillets lengthwise, three quarters of the way through each one, and open them out as flat as possible.
4 Spread one piece of meat with half the stuffing, then cover with another fillet. Spread the remaining stuffing over the top and cover with the remaining fillet.
5 Stretch the streaky bacon rashers with the back of a knife, then wrap them round the meat and tie with string to form a 'joint'.
6 Place the meat in a roasting pan. Pour the wine around the base and brush the meat with the oil. Bake for 1 ½-2 hours. Serve with roast potatoes and steamed vegetables, such as broccoli or carrots.

Note: The cooking juices can be thickened with a little cornflour and served with the pork, if wished.

MEAT AND APPLE BAKES

Serves 4

225 g/8 oz bread, crusts removed
225 g/8 oz cooked meat, such as pork, lamb or beef
1 onion, chopped
2 eating apples, peeled, cored and grated
salt and pepper

450 ml/15 fl oz beef stock
5 ml/1 tsp dried mixed herbs
dash of Worcestershire sauce
15 g/½ oz butter or margarine

METHOD

1 Preheat the oven to 190°C/375°F/GAS MARK 5.
2 Dice the bread. Mix together the cooked meat, onion and grated apple. Season with salt and pepper.
3 Spread half the bread in the bottom of a pie dish. Spoon the meat mixture on top and cover with the rest of the bread.
4 Mix the stock, herbs and Worcestershire sauce, then pour it over the bread. Dot with the butter and bake for 45 minutes. Serve with a mixed salad or julienne strips of carrots and courgettes.

Stuffed Pork Fillet

MEAT LOAF

Serves 8-10

450 g/1 lb lean pork, minced
2 onions, chopped
1 garlic clove, crushed
225 g/8 oz sausagemeat
100 g/4 oz fresh breadcrumbs
1 egg, beaten
15 ml/1 tbsp chopped fresh sage
15 ml/1 tbsp chopped fresh parsley
salt and pepper
8-10 streaky bacon rashers, rinded

METHOD

1 Preheat the oven to 190°C/375°F/GAS MARK 5.
2 Place the minced pork, onions, garlic, sausagemeat, breadcrumbs, egg, herbs and salt and pepper in a bowl and mix well.
3 Lay the bacon rashers on a board and, using the back of a knife, stretch the rashers until almost doubled in length. Use to line the base and sides of a 900 g/2 lb loaf tin.
4 Spoon the pork mixture into the lined tin and smooth the surface. Fold the excess bacon over the top of the pork mixture.
5 Cover tightly with foil and place in a roasting tin half filled with cold water. Cook for 1 ½ hours.
6 Leave to cool in the tin, then chill overnight. Turn out and serve sliced with salad.

PORK HOTPOT

Serves 4

450 g/1 lb lean pork, cut into small cubes
2 onions, sliced
225 g/8 oz carrots, thinly sliced
450 g/1 lb potatoes, sliced
450 ml/15 fl oz stock
30 ml/2 tbsp chopped fresh herbs or 10 ml/2 tsp dried mixed herbs
salt and pepper

METHOD

1 Preheat the oven to 180°C/350°F/GAS MARK 4.
2 Fry the pork cubes in a pan over high heat until the fat runs.
3 Arrange a layer of onion slices in the base of a casserole. Cover with a layer of meat and a sprinkling of herbs, then a layer of carrots. Top with a layer of potato slices.
4 Repeat the layers until all the ingredients are used up, finishing with a layer of potato slices. Season with salt and pepper and pour the stock over the top. Cover with greased greaseproof paper.
5 Cook for 1 hour, then remove the paper and cook for another 30-60 minutes, until the top is brown and the meat is tender.

Meat Loaf

RAISED PORK PIE

Serves 4-6

For the pastry:

150 ml/5 fl oz milk

50 g/2 oz lard

225 g/8 oz plain flour

salt and pepper

beaten egg, to glaze

For the filling:

700 g/1 ½ lb sausagemeat

225 g/8 oz streaky bacon, rinded and chopped

1 onion, chopped

10 ml/2 tsp dried mixed herbs

METHOD

1 Heat the milk and lard in a pan until the lard melts. Bring to the boil. Mix the flour and 2.5 ml/½ tsp salt in a bowl and make a well in the centre. Pour in the hot liquid and beat with a wooden spoon, then knead for a few seconds to form a silky dough. Cover with clingfilm and leave to rest for 10 minutes. Do not allow it to cool. Preheat the oven to 220°C/425°F/GAS MARK 4. Grease a 900 g/2 lb loaf tin.

2 To make the filling, mix together the sausagemeat, bacon, onion, mixed herbs and salt and pepper.

3 Roll out the pastry and use to line the loaf tin, reserving enough pastry to make a lid. Spoon the filling into the tin. Cover with the remaining pastry. Brush with beaten egg. Decorate with the pastry trimmings.

4 Bake for about 1 hour, until cooked through. Turn out of the tin and serve hot or cold.

SAUSAGE AND BACON PLAIT
Serves 4-6

250 g/9 oz ready-made shortcrust pastry
beaten egg, to glaze

For the filling:

225 g/8 oz sausagemeat
225 g/8 oz back bacon, rinded and chopped
2 eggs, hard-boiled and sliced or chopped

2 leeks, trimmed and finely chopped
5 ml/1 tsp dried sage or oregano
salt and pepper

METHOD
1 Preheat the oven to 200°C/400°F/GAS MARK 6.
2 On a lightly floured surface, roll out the pastry to a 30 cm/12 in square.
3 Mix all the filling ingredients together in a bowl. Spoon the mixture down the centre one third of the pastry, leaving the sides clear.
4 Brush the uncovered pastry with beaten egg and cut into diagonal slices about 12 mm/½ in thick. Lift strips from each side alternately and place over the filling to form a roll resembling a plait.
5 Brush the pastry with beaten egg and bake for 45-60 minutes.

Variation: Replace the leeks with onion.

BACON AND ONION PIE

Serves 4

250 g/9 oz ready-made shortcrust pastry
beaten egg, to glaze

For the filling:

2 onions, chopped
1 large cooking apple, peeled, cored and sliced
50 g/2 oz Cheddar cheese, grated
225 g/8 oz streaky bacon, rinded and diced

25 g/1 oz plain flour
150 ml/5 fl oz chicken or vegetable stock
salt and pepper

METHOD

1 Preheat the oven to 190°C/375°F/GAS MARK 5.
2 To make the filling, place the onions in the base of a 1.2 litre/2 pint ovenproof dish. Arrange the apple slices over the top.
3 Sprinkle the cheese over the apple and cover that with the diced bacon. Blend the flour and stock. Season with salt and pepper, and pour it over the filling.
4 On a lightly floured surface, roll out the pastry 5 cm/2 in wider than the dish. Cut a 2.5 cm/1 in wide strip from the outer edge.Dampen the rim of the dish and place the pastry strip on it.
5 Lift the remaining pastry on the rolling pin and lay it over the dish. Press the lid lightly on to the rim to seal. Flute the edges.
6 Make a diagonal cross in the centre of the pastry lid, then fold back the pastry to reveal the filling. Brush the pastry with beaten egg to glaze. Bake for 45 minutes. Serve hot or cold.

EGG AND BACON PIE

Serves 4

250 g/9 oz ready-made shortcrust pastry
milk, to glaze

For the filling:

25 g/1 oz butter
225 g/8 oz lean back bacon, rinded and diced
1 onion, chopped

4 eggs
15-30 ml/1-2 tbsp chopped fresh parsley
pepper

METHOD

1 To make the filling, melt the butter in a frying pan and fry the bacon and onion for 5 minutes, stirring. Leave to cool slightly.
2 Preheat the oven to 190°C/375°F/GAS MARK 5. On a lightly floured surface, roll out two thirds of the pastry and use to line a 20 cm/8 in flan tin set on a baking sheet. Fill with the bacon and onion.
3 Make four wells in the bacon and onion mixture. Break one egg at a time into a cup, then place one in each well. Sprinkle the parsley over the top and season with pepper.
4 Roll out the remaining pastry to make a lid. Dampen the pastry edges in the tin and cover with the pastry round. Seal the edges well together and trim neatly. Re-roll the trimmings and use to decorate the pie.
5 Brush the pastry surface with milk and bake for 45 minutes, until golden brown. Serve hot or cold.

Bacon and Onion Pie

SAUSAGE AND CAULIFLOWER PUDDING

Serves 4-6

For the pudding:

450 g/1 lb herby sausages
1 onion, chopped
100 g/4 oz mushrooms, chopped
30 ml/2 tbsp chopped fresh chives

1 large egg, beaten
50 g/2 oz breadcrumbs
salt and pepper
1 small cauliflower, broken into florets

For the sauce:

25 g/1 oz butter
25 g/1 oz plain flour
300 ml/10 fl oz beef stock

METHOD

1 Grease a 1.2 litre/2 pint pudding basin.
2 Skin the sausages, then mix the sausage meat with the onion, mushrooms and chives.
3 Add the beaten egg and breadcrumbs, and season with salt and pepper. Mix together thoroughly.
4 Place some of the sausage mixture in the bottom of the greased pudding basin, then arrange a layer of cauliflower on top. Continue alternating layers of sausage mixture and cauliflower, finishing with a layer of sausage mixture.
5 Cover the pudding basin with greased greaseproof paper with a pleat down the centre to allow for expansion and a pudding cloth or foil. Boil or steam for 1 ½-2 hours.
6 Just before the pudding is ready, make the brown sauce. Melt the butter in a pan and add the flour. Cook for 1 minute or until the butter and flour mixture is slightly brown, stirring constantly. Add the stock and bring to the boil, then reduce the heat and cook, stirring, until the sauce thickens.
7 Turn out the pudding on to a warmed serving dish and serve with the brown sauce and a selection of baby vegetables.

Variations: For a more colourful pudding, use broccoli instead of cauliflower and serve with a home-made tomato sauce (*see* **Note**, Bacon Roly Poly).

BACON ROLY POLY

Serves 4

For the pastry:

225 g/8 oz self-raising flour
good pinch of salt

100 g/4 oz shredded suet
beaten egg, to glaze

For the filling:

225 g/8 oz lean bacon rashers, rinded and chopped
1 onion, chopped
1 carrot, chopped

1 stick celery, chopped
50 g/2 oz mushrooms, chopped
salt and pepper

METHOD

1 Preheat the oven to 190°C/375°F/GAS MARK 5.
2 To make the pastry, sift the flour and the pinch of salt into a bowl and stir in the shredded suet. Add

Bacon Roly Poly

135 ml/9 tbsp cold water and mix gently to form a fairly soft dough. Knead the dough lightly.

3 Mix all the filling ingredients together in a large bowl.

4 On a lightly floured surface, roll out the pastry to an oblong measuring 25 x 30 cm/10 x 12 in. Spread the filling over the pastry to within 12 mm/½ in of the edges.

5 Brush the edges with beaten egg, then turn them in. Brush the turned-in edges with beaten egg and roll up the pastry, starting at a short side.

6 Place the roll, join side down, on a baking tray. Brush with beaten egg and cook for about 25 minutes, until golden brown. Cover with foil to prevent overbrowning and continue cooking for another 20 minutes, or until cooked through. Serve hot with a salad or vegetables.

Note: This particularly good served with a home-made tomato sauce. For a quick sauce, mix together a 400 g/14 oz can chopped tomatoes, 15-30 ml/1-2 tbsp chopped fresh herbs, 15 ml/1 tbsp tomato purée, 15 ml/1 tbsp tomato ketchup, 1 crushed garlic clove, 150 ml/5 fl oz white wine and salt and pepper. Bring to the boil and simmer for a few minutes. Purée it in a blender or food processor if you want a completely smooth sauce.

GLORIA'S MUSHROOM CHICKEN

Serves 4

50 g/2 oz butter
4 skinless chicken breasts
2 onions, sliced
2 garlic cloves, crushed
225 g/8 oz mushrooms
300 ml/10 fl oz milk

295 g/10 oz can condensed mushroom soup
15 ml/1 tbsp tomato purée
dash of Tabasco sauce
dash of sherry (optional)
salt and pepper

METHOD

1 Preheat the oven to 180°C/350°F/gas 4.
2 Melt the butter in a pan and brown the chicken breasts all over. Remove from the pan with a slotted spoon and arrange in an ovenproof dish. Fry the onions and garlic in the fat remaining in the pan until the onions are translucent.
3 Add the mushrooms and cook for 2-3 minutes. Add the milk and simmer gently for 3 minutes, then add the soup, tomato purée, Tabasco sauce and sherry, if using. Season with salt and pepper.
4 Pour the sauce over the chicken, cover the dish and cook for about 1 hour, until the chicken is cooked and tender.

Variation: This sauce is equally good served with fish or prawns.

CHICKEN CASSEROLE

Serves 4-6

50 g/2 oz butter
1 large onion, sliced
1.8 kg/4 lb oven-ready chicken
6 carrots, sliced

4 sticks celery, sliced
bouquet garni
salt and pepper
225 g/8 oz mushrooms, sliced

METHOD

1 Melt the butter in a large pan and fry the onion and the whole chicken for about 10 minutes, until the chicken is browned on all sides.
2 Add the carrots, celery, bouquet garni and salt and pepper. Add enough water to just cover the chicken. Bring to the boil, reduce the heat and simmer for 1 ½ hours.
3 Preheat the oven to 180°C/350°F/GAS MARK 4.
4 Remove the chicken and, when cool enough, cut it into small pieces. Strain the cooking liquid, reserving the vegetables. Measure 900 ml/1 ½ pints of the cooking liquid and place it in a pan (the remaining cooking liquid can be cooled and frozen to use as stock). Blend the cornflour with a little water and stir it into the liquid in the pan. Cook until the mixture thickens and then simmer for 3 minutes.
5 Add the chicken pieces, cooked vegetables and mushrooms and transfer to an ovenproof dish. Cook in the oven for 45 minutes. Serve with cooked rice or potatoes.

Variations: Green pepper or sliced beans can be added to the casserole. The casserole can be cooked ahead and then reheated, if preferred.

Chicken Casserole

MACKEREL IN PARCHMENT

Serves 4

4 mackerel (or 8, if small)
5 ml/1 tsp made English mustard
1 lemon
salt and pepper

15-30 ml/1-2 tbsp chopped fresh parsley
4 spring onions, quartered and cut into thin strips
1 large tomato, skinned, seeded and cut into thin strips
parsley sprigs and lemon wedges, to garnish (optional)

METHOD

1 Preheat the oven to 180°C/350°F/GAS MARK 4. Cut out four pieces of baking parchment or greaseproof paper large enough to hold the mackerel and grease them lightly.

2 Gut the fish, cut off the heads and fins and remove the backbones. Open out each fish flat and place them skin side down on the squares of baking parchment or greaseproof paper.

3 Spread each fish with mustard. Add a squeeze of lemon juice, salt and pepper and a little chopped parsley.

4 Fold each fish over to re-form the shape. Sprinkle with strips of spring onion and tomato, and add another squeeze of lemon juice.

5 Seal each paper parcel and bake for 20-25 minutes, or until the fish is cooked through. Unwrap the parcels and insert sprigs of parsley and lemon wedges to garnish, if wished. Serve in the paper parcels.

PLAICE AND PRAWN ROLLS

Serves 4

8 plaice fillets, skinned and boned
about ¼ bunch watercress, trimmed
   and separated into leaves
1 shallot, finely chopped
salt and pepper
16 cooked peeled prawns
50 g/2 oz butter

15 ml/1 tbsp lemon juice
60 ml/4 tbsp dry white wine
30 ml/2 tbsp plain flour
300 ml/10 fl oz fish stock
40 g/1 ½ oz Cheddar cheese, grated
60 ml/4 tbsp double cream
dill sprigs and lettuce leaves, to garnish

METHOD

1 Preheat the oven to 190°C/375°F/GAS MARK 5. Lay the fish fillets on a board and cover each one with a few watercress leaves and chopped shallot. Season with salt and pepper. Place two prawns at one end of each fillet. Form into neat rolls and secure with cocktail sticks. Melt 25 g/1 oz butter in a frying pan, add the fish rolls, lemon juice and wine. Cover and poach gently for about 3 minutes, until the fish is just tender. Lift the rolls into a shallow ovenproof dish and remove the cocktail sticks. Reserve the liquid.

2 Melt the remaining butter in a pan, stir in the flour and cook for 1 minute. Stir in the reserved cooking liquid and the stock. Bring to the boil, stirring, then reduce the heat and simmer for 2 minutes.

3 Remove from the heat and stir in the cheese and the cream. Pour the sauce over the fish rolls and cook in the oven for 15-20 minutes, until lightly browned. Serve garnished with sprigs of dill and lettuce leaves.

MUSSEL STEW

Serves 4

48 mussels in their shells
450 ml/15 fl oz dry white wine
75 g/3 oz butter
4 rashers smoked bacon, rinded
  and cut into slivers
2 leeks, quartered and thinly sliced
1-2 garlic cloves, crushed
2 sticks celery, trimmed and chopped

1 small red pepper, seeded and diced
45 ml/3 tbsp plain flour
900 ml/1 ½ pints chicken stock
2 good pinches of saffron strands, finely crushed
300 ml/10 fl oz double cream
salt and pepper
45 ml/3 tbsp chopped fresh chives
45 ml/3 tbsp chopped fresh parsley or dill

METHOD

1 Scrub the mussels and remove the beards. Discard any damaged mussels and any that are open and do not close when sharply tapped with the back of a knife.

2 Place the mussels in a large pan with the wine and bring to the boil. Cover and cook for 3-4 minutes, shaking the pan frequently until the mussels open. Remove from the heat, strain the cooking liquid and reserve it. Discard any mussels that have not opened.

3 Melt the butter in a pan, add the bacon, leeks, garlic, celery and red pepper and fry gently for 5 minutes, stirring frequently. Stir in the flour and cook for 1 minute. Gradually stir in the stock. Add the saffron and the reserved cooking liquid, cover and simmer gently for 20 minutes.

4 Stir in half the cream and the mussels. Season with salt and pepper. Scatter half the chives and parsley over the top.

5 Serve hot with the remaining cream and herbs drizzled over the top, accompanied by crusty bread.

Note: This is an easy recipe to double up when you want to feed large numbers of people.

FISH IN BATTER

Serves 4

50 g/2 oz plain flour
pinch of salt
1 egg
milk

vegetable oil for deep frying
450 g/1 lb cod fillet, cut into
4 cm/1 ½ in squares
parsley sprigs, to garnish

METHOD

1 Sift the flour and salt into a bowl and make a well in the centre. Add the egg to the well, then gradually work to a thick batter, adding a little milk. Beat well and add enough milk to the batter to thin down to a coating consistency.

2 Heat the oil in a deep fat fryer. Dip the fish pieces in batter, then fry, a few at a time, in the hot fat until golden brown all over.

3 Serve the fish on a warm dish, garnished with parsley sprigs.

Mussel Stew

FISH CREAM

Serves 4

450 g/1 lb cooked cod fillet, skinned and boned
100 g/4 oz fresh breadcrumbs
300 ml/10 fl oz milk
25 g/1 oz butter
salt and pepper
2 eggs, separated
squeeze of lemon juice
175 g/6 oz mushrooms, sliced
200 g/7 oz can sweetcorn kernels
30 ml/2 tbsp chopped fresh parsley

METHOD

1 Preheat the oven to 200°C/400°F/GAS MARK 6. Grease a 1.7 litre/3 pint ovenproof dish.
2 Flake the fish into a pan and add the breadcrumbs, milk and butter. Season with salt and pepper. Cook over gentle heat for about 5 minutes.
3 Beat the egg yolks, then add them to the fish with the lemon juice, mushrooms, sweetcorn and parsley. Mix well.
4 Whisk the egg whites until stiff, then fold them into the mixture. Pour the mixture into the dish and bake for 25–30 minutes, until lightly browned on top. Serve with jacket or new potatoes and peas or carrots.

HERRINGS IN OATMEAL

Serves 4

4 herrings (about 175 g/6 oz each), cleaned and boned with heads and tails removed
salt and pepper
75 g/3 oz fine or medium oatmeal
generous pinch of freshly grated nutmeg
50 g/2 oz butter
chopped fresh parsley and lemon wedges, to serve

METHOD

1 Season the herrings generously with salt and pepper. Mix the oatmeal with the nutmeg and turn the herrings in the mixture, pressing well until they are coated.
2 Melt the butter in a frying pan, add the fish and cook over moderate heat for about 5–7 minutes on each side, until crisp and cooked through.
3 Remove the fish with a fish slice, drain and serve immediately, sprinkled with the parsley and accompanied by the lemon wedges. Serve with crusty bread and a mixed salad.

Note: Herrings taste good served with an anchovy sauce. Make up a 300 ml/10 fl oz quantity of white sauce, then add 10 ml/2 tsp anchovy essence and a squeeze of lemon juice. Season with pepper.

Variation: The fish may be cooked under a medium grill, if preferred.

SMOKED FISH AND PRAWN PIE

Serves 4

For the topping:

900 g/2 lb potatoes, cut into chunks
salt and pepper
60 g/2 ½ oz butter
1 leek, chopped
1 small onion, chopped

For the fish mixture:

450 g/1 lb smoked cod or haddock
450 ml/15 fl oz milk
25 g/1 oz butter
25 g/1 oz plain flour
30-45 ml/2-3 tbsp chopped fresh parsley
100 g/4 oz cooked peeled prawns
40 g/1 ½ oz Cheddar cheese, grated

METHOD

1 Preheat the oven to 200°C/400°F/GAS MARK 6.

2 Cook the potatoes in boiling salted water until tender. Drain well, return to the pan and shake over a low heat to dry them. Mash with 40 g/1 ½ oz of the butter. Season with salt and pepper.

3 Melt the remaining butter for the topping in a pan, add the leek and onion and fry gently for 5 minutes, stirring frequently. Stir into the potato and mix well.

4 Place the fish in a pan, add the milk and cook gently for 10 minutes. Drain the cooked fish, reserving 300 ml/10 fl oz of the milk. Allow the fish to cool slightly until cool enough to handle, then flake it, discarding the skin and bones.

5 Melt the 25 g/1 oz butter in a pan, stir in the flour and cook for 1 minute. Gradually stir in the reserved milk and bring to the boil, stirring, then simmer for 2 minutes. Remove from the heat.

6 Stir in the flaked fish, parsley and prawns and season to taste with salt and pepper. Spoon the mixture into an ovenproof dish and cover with the potato mixture, marking it in an attractive pattern with a fork. Sprinkle the grated Cheddar cheese over the top. Bake for about 40 minutes, until the topping is golden brown. Serve hot.

Variations: Substitute unsmoked fish, such as cod or haddock, for the smoked fish or, for special occasions, salmon or monkfish. Replace the Cheddar cheese with another hard cheese, if preferred, or omit it altogether.

FISH AND POTATO BAKE

Serves 4

450 g/1 lb cod fillets, cut into pieces
25 g/1 oz fine oatmeal
salt and pepper
450 g/1 lb potatoes, thinly sliced
1 onion, sliced
175 g/6 oz mushrooms, sliced
2 eggs, hard-boiled and sliced

15 ml/1 tbsp chopped fresh tarragon
25 g/1 oz butter or margarine
25 g/1 oz plain flour
450 ml/15 fl oz milk
75 g/3 oz Cheddar cheese, grated
flat-leaf parsley sprigs, to garnish

METHOD

1 Preheat the oven to 190°C/375°C/GAS MARK 5.
2 Mix together the fish, oatmeal and seasoning, until the fish is coated with the oatmeal.
3 Cook the potatoes in boiling water for 5 minutes, then drain.
4 Place the fish in the base of an ovenproof dish. Arrange the onion, mushrooms, eggs and tarragon over the fish. Cover with the potato slices.
5 Melt the butter in a pan, add the flour and cook for 1 minute. Gradually add the milk and bring to the boil, stirring, until the mixture thickens. Simmer for 2 minutes. Remove from the heat, season with salt and pepper and stir in 50 g/2 oz of the cheese.
6 Pour the sauce over the potatoes and sprinkle with the remaining cheese. Cover with foil and bake for 45 minutes. Brown the topping under the grill before serving.
7 Garnish with flat-leaf parsley and serve with steamed baby vegetables, broccoli, spring cabbage, grilled tomatoes or sweetcorn, or with a tossed side salad and crusty bread.

FISH FILLETS WITH MUSHROOM SAUCE

Serves 4

4 white fish fillets, such as lemon
sole, cod or haddock
15 ml/1 tbsp chopped fresh herbs or
5 ml/1 tsp dried mixed herbs

salt and pepper
295 g/10 oz can condensed mushroom soup
50-75 g/2-3 oz Cheddar cheese, grated

METHOD

1 Preheat the oven to 180°C/350°F/GAS MARK 4. Grease an ovenproof dish.
2 Arrange the fish fillets in the dish. Season with salt and pepper and sprinkle with the herbs.
3 Pour the soup over the fish and sprinkle the grated cheese over the top. Cook for 30 minutes, or until the fish is tender.

Fish and Potato Bake

SMOKED FISH PUFF PARCELS

Serves 4

350 g/12 oz ready-made puff pastry
beaten egg, to glaze

For the filling:

350 g/12 oz cooked smoked fish
(haddock or cod), flaked and boned
100 g/4 oz small cooked peeled prawns
225 g/8 oz mashed potatoes
25 g/1 oz butter, melted

30 ml/2 tbsp chopped fresh parsley or tarragon
few drops of anchovy essence
salt and pepper
1 egg, beaten

METHOD

1 Preheat the oven to 220°C/425°F/GAS MARK 7. To make the filling, mix together the fish, prawns, potatoes, butter, parsley, anchovy essence, salt and pepper and beaten egg.

2 Divide the pastry into four. On a lightly floured surface, roll out each piece to a 20 cm/8 in square or circle. Spoon a quarter of the filling onto the centre of each pastry square or circle. Dampen the pastry edges and fold it over to enclose the filling and make a parcel. Place the parcels on a baking sheet.

3 Brush with beaten egg and score the tops of the parcels. Bake for 25–30 minutes, until golden brown.

IRISHMAN'S OMELETTE

Serves 2

25 g/1 oz butter
100 g/4 oz streaky bacon rashers,
rinded and chopped
1 small onion, chopped
1 large potato, cooked and diced

50 g/2 oz cabbage, shredded
3-4 eggs
15 ml/1 tbsp chopped fresh herbs
salt and pepper

METHOD

1 Heat the butter in a large non-stick frying pan. Add the bacon, onion, potato and cabbage and fry, stirring from time to time, for 8-10 minutes, until the bacon and onion are cooked.

2 In a bowl, beat the eggs just enough to break them down. Add the herbs and season with salt and pepper.

3 Stir the eggs into the pan and cook over a gentle heat until the eggs set.

4 Place the pan under a preheated grill until the omelette is golden brown on top. Serve with crusty bread, new or jacket potatoes and grilled or sliced tomatoes.

VEGETABLE PIE

Serves 4

175 g/6 oz ready-made shortcrust pastry
beaten egg, to glaze

For the filling:

40 g/1 ½ oz butter
225 g/8 oz carrots, thinly sliced
225 g/8 oz swede or turnips, diced
1 onion, sliced
40 g/1 ½ oz plain flour
300 ml/10 fl oz vegetable stock

1 small cauliflower, broken into
florets and blanched
100 g/4 oz frozen broad beans
30 ml/2 tbsp chopped fresh parsley
salt and pepper

METHOD

1 Preheat the oven to 200°C/400°F/GAS MARK 6.

2 To make the filling, melt the butter in a pan and fry the carrots, swede and onion for 8 minutes. Add the flour and cook for 1 minute.

3 Gradually add the stock, bring to the boil, stirring continuously, and simmer for 2 minutes. Add the cauliflower, beans, parsley and salt and pepper, and mix well.

4 On a lightly floured surface, roll out the pastry 5 cm/2 in wider than a 900 ml–1.2 litre/1 ½–2 pint pie dish. Cut a 2.5 cm/1 in wide strip from the outer edge. Dampen the rim of the dish and place the pastry strip on it.

5 Spoon the vegetable mixture into the dish. Lift the remaining pastry on the rolling pin and lay it over the pie dish. Press the lid lightly on to the rim to seal. Scallop the edges, if wished. Roll out the pastry trimmings and use to decorate the pie. Brush with beaten egg and cut a slit in the centre to allow the steam to escape. Bake for 45 minutes.

CHEESE AND POTATO FLAN

Serves 4–6

175 g/6 oz ready-made shortcrust pastry
25 g/1 oz butter or margarine
2 sticks celery, chopped
1 small onion, chopped
25 g/1 oz plain flour

300 ml/10 fl oz milk
100 g/4 oz cheese, grated
salt and pepper
225 g/8 oz cubed cooked potato
25 g/1 oz fresh breadcrumbs

METHOD

1 Preheat the oven to 200°C/400°F/GAS MARK 6.

2 On a lightly floured surface, roll out the pastry and use to line a 21.5 cm/8 ½ in flan tin. Bake blind for 10 minutes. Remove the baking beans and paper and bake for a further 10–15 minutes.

3 Meanwhile, melt the butter in a pan and sauté the celery and onion for 5 minutes. Add the flour and cook for 1 minute. Gradually stir in the milk, bring slowly to the boil, stirring, then simmer for 3 minutes.

4 Remove the sauce from the heat and stir in the cheese. Season with salt and pepper. Add the cooked potato and mix well.

5 Place the mixture in the flan case, sprinkle the breadcrumbs over the top and bake for 15–20 minutes, until lightly browned on top. Serve hot or cold.

Vegetable Pie

PUDDINGS

'When I think of childhood, it's those wonderful kitchen smells which evoke so many memories.'

Favourite Hunniford family puddings include fresh fruit pies, Lena's apple cake and steamed puddings – everything from orange pudding to wartime plum pudding. Thick Irish cream was used to make rich syllabubs, and buttermilk was added to pancake batter.

ORANGE PUDDING

Serves 4

For the pudding:
100 g/4 oz sugar
100 g/4 oz butter or margarine
finely grated zest of 2 oranges
2 eggs, beaten
175 g/6 oz self-raising flour
a little milk

For the orange sauce:
300 g/10 oz marmalade
juice of 2 oranges

METHOD

1 Cream the sugar and butter until pale and fluffy. Add the grated zest and beaten eggs. Fold in the flour. Add enough milk to make a dropping consistency.
2 Turn the mixture in to a greased 900 ml/1 ½ pint pudding basin, cover with a double layer of greased greaseproof paper, with a pleat down the centre to allow for expansion, and a pudding cloth or foil. Steam for 1 ½ hours.
3 Just before the pudding is ready, make the sauce. Melt the marmalade in a pan with the orange juice, bring to the boil, stirring continuously, and boil for 1 minute. Sieve and serve hot with the pudding.

Variations: For a sharper sauce, replace the oranges with lemons or one lemon and one lime.

SPICY PEACH SPONGE PUDDING

Serves 4

410 g/14 oz can peach halves or slices, drained
5 ml/1 tsp ground cinnamon
100 g/4 oz butter or margarine
100 g/4 oz caster sugar
2 eggs, beaten
175 g/6 oz self-raising flour
a little milk
50 g/2 oz chopped walnuts

METHOD

1 Preheat the oven to 180°C/350°F/GAS MARK 4. Grease a shallow ovenproof dish.
2 Arrange the peaches in a single layer in the bottom of the dish and sprinkle with the cinnamon.
3 Cream the butter and sugar together, then gradually add the beaten eggs. Fold in the flour and add enough milk to make a soft dropping consistency.
4 Spread the mixture over the peaches and sprinkle the chopped walnuts on top.
5 Bake for 35-40 minutes, then serve warm with cream or custard.

Orange Pudding

LENA'S APPLE CAKE

Serves 4-6

100 g/4 oz soft brown sugar
100 g/4 oz butter or margarine
2 eggs, beaten
225 g/8 oz self-raising flour
5 ml/1 tsp baking powder

5 ml/1 tsp mixed spice
pinch of salt
1 large cooking apple, peeled and cored
about 30 ml/2 tbsp milk, to mix

For the topping:
45 ml/3 tbsp demerara or soft brown sugar
2.5 ml/½ tsp mixed spice

METHOD

1 Preheat the oven to 180°C/350°F/GAS MARK 4. Grease a 20 cm/8 in deep round cake tin or an 18 cm/7 in square tin.
2 Cream the sugar and butter. Add the eggs and fold in the flour, baking powder, mixed spice and salt. Chop half the apple and stir into the mixture. Add enough milk to give a soft dropping consistency.
3 Turn the mixture into the cake tin and level the surface. Cut the remaining apple into thin slices and arrange them over the top of the cake.
4 To make the topping, mix together the demerara sugar and mixed spice. Sprinkle it over the apple slices. Bake for about 1 ½ hours. Serve hot or cold, cut into wedges or squares, with cream or ice cream.

IMPERIAL PUDDING

Serves 4

For the pastry:
25 g/1 oz butter or margarine
225 g/8 oz plain flour
50 g/2 oz shredded suet

2.5 ml/½ tsp salt
2.5 ml/½ tsp baking powder
1 raw potato

For the filling:
1-2 apples
50 g/2 oz currants or raisins

15 ml/1 tbsp golden syrup
few drops of lemon essence

METHOD

1 Grease a 1.2 litre/2 pint pudding basin. To make the pastry, rub the butter into the flour, then mix in the suet, salt, baking powder and grated potato. Add enough cold water to mix to a stiff paste.
2 To make the filling, grate the apples and mix with the dried fruit, syrup and lemon essence.
3 Divide the pastry into four. Roll out one piece large enough to fit in the bottom of the pudding basin. Cover it with one third of the filling, keeping it away from the edges of the pastry. Brush the uncovered pastry edges with water.
4 Roll out the second piece of pastry, large enough to cover the filling. Place it in the pudding basin, pressing it onto the first layer of pastry. Repeat the layers until all the filling and pastry is used, finishing with a layer of pastry.
5 Cover the pudding basin with greased greaseproof paper, with a pleat down the centre to allow for expansion, and a pudding cloth or foil. Steam for 1 ½-2 hours.

Lena's Apple Cake

WARTIME PLUM PUDDING

Serves 4-6

225 g/8 oz self-raising flour
pinch of salt
5 ml/1 tsp baking powder
50 g/2 oz butter or margarine
175 g/6 oz dried fruit
5 ml/1 tsp cocoa powder
10 ml/2 tsp mixed spice
50 g/2 oz sugar
25 g/1 oz grated raw carrot
25 g/1 oz grated raw potato
2 eggs, beaten
about 45 ml/3 tbsp milk

METHOD

1 Sift the flour, salt and baking powder into a bowl. Rub the butter into the flour.
2 Mix the fruit with the cocoa powder and the mixed spice. Add the fruit and the sugar to the flour mixture. Mix well. Stir in the grated carrot and potato. Add the beaten eggs and mix well. Add enough milk to make a dropping consistency.
3 Turn in to a greased 1.3 litre/2 ½ pint pudding basin, cover with a double layer of greased greaseproof paper, with a pleat down the centre to allow for expansion, and a pudding cloth or foil. Steam for 1 ½-2 hours. Serve with brandy butter or sauce.

Variations: Add the finely grated zest of 1 orange or lemon. Replace 75 g/3 oz of the dried fruit with chopped dried apricots. Add ground cinnamon or ginger instead of the mixed spice.

IRISH PANCAKES

Serves 6-8

225 g/8 oz self-raising flour
50 g/2 oz sugar
2 eggs, well beaten
225 ml/8 fl oz milk and buttermilk, mixed
vegetable oil for frying
sugar and lemon juice, to serve

METHOD

1 Sift the flour into a bowl and stir in the sugar. Make a well in the centre and add the well beaten eggs and the milk and buttermilk. Beat well, drawing in the flour from the sides to make a smooth batter.
2 Heat a little oil in an 18 cm/7 in heavy-based frying pan. Pour in enough batter to coat the base of the pan. Cook for 1-2 minutes, until golden brown, then turn or toss, and cook the other side until golden. Keep warm while cooking the rest.
3 Serve hot, sprinkled with sugar and lemon juice.

Wartime Plum Pudding

FRESH FRUIT JELLY
Serves 4-6

20 ml/4 tsp powdered gelatine
600 ml/1 pint unsweetened apple juice
50 g/2 oz caster sugar
150 ml/5 fl oz dry or medium white wine
450 g/1 lb fresh prepared fruit, such as strawberries, raspberries and blackberries

METHOD
1 Sprinkle the gelatine over 4 tbsp water in a small bowl and leave to soften. Stand the bowl over a pan of simmering water and stir until the gelatine has dissolved. Cool slightly.
2 Place the apple juice and sugar in a saucepan and heat gently until the sugar has dissolved. Remove the pan from the heat and stir in the gelatine and wine, mixing well.
3 Place the prepared fruit in a 1.4 litre/2 ½ pint jelly mould. Strain the juice mixture over the fruit in the jelly mould.
4 Allow to cool, then chill in the refrigerator until the mixture is syrupy. Stir to distribute the fruit evenly, then chill until set.
5 To serve, carefully turn out onto a plate and serve on its own or with fresh fruit.

VANILLA TABLE CREAM
Serves 4

2 eggs, separated
40 g/1 ½ oz caster sugar
600 ml/1 pint milk
few drops of vanilla essence
15 g/½ oz powdered gelatine

METHOD
1 Beat the egg yolks, sugar and 45 ml/3 tbsp of the milk in a bowl until smooth. Bring the rest of the milk to the boil in a pan.
2 Pour the hot milk onto the egg yolks, then strain the mixture into the top of a double boiler or into a heavy-based saucepan. Cook, stirring, until the custard thickens slightly. Do not allow it to boil. Stir in the vanilla essence.
3 Sprinkle the gelatine over 30 ml/2 tbsp water in a small bowl and leave to soften. Stand the bowl over a pan of simmering water and stir until the gelatine has dissolved. Stir the gelatine into the custard, then leave it to cool.
4 Whisk the egg whites until stiff, then fold them into the cooled custard. Pour the mixture into a wetted 1.2 litre/2 pint mould and chill in the refrigerator until set. Turn out to serve.

Note: It is important to soak the gelatine for a few minutes in a small amount of cold water, until it is soft and spongy, then it will dissolve without any lumps. Always sprinkle the powdered gelatine over the water, not the water over the gelatine.

ORANGE SYLLABUB
Serves 4-6

grated zest and juice of 1 orange
150 ml/5 fl oz sweet white wine
30 ml/2 tbsp brandy
25 g/1 oz caster sugar
300 ml/10 fl oz double cream

METHOD

1 Mix together the orange zest and juice, white wine, brandy and caster sugar in a large bowl. Stir until the sugar has dissolved.
2 Pour in the double cream and whip the mixture until it forms soft peaks. Spoon into individual glasses and chill in the refrigerator before serving.

RAISIN AND WALNUT ICE CREAM
Serves 4-6

75 g/3 oz raisins, chopped roughly
60 ml/4 tbsp whiskey
3 egg yolks
75 g/3 oz caster sugar
300 ml/10 fl oz milk
300 ml/10 fl oz double cream
75 g/3 oz walnuts, chopped

METHOD

1 Set the freezer to maximum or fast freeze about 1 hour beforehand. Soak the raisins in the whiskey for 30 minutes.
2 Beat the egg yolks and sugar in a bowl until well blended. Stir in the milk, mix well, then strain into a pan. Heat gently over a low heat until the custard coats the back of the spoon. Do not boil. Pour into a chilled bowl and allow to cool.
3 Whisk the cream into the cold custard and fold in the raisins, whisky and walnuts.
4 Pour into a 1 litre/1 ¾ pint freeezer container, cover and and freeze for about 3 hours, or until mushy in consistency. Stir to distribute the raisins and walnuts evenly. Return to the freezer and freeze until firm.
5 Transfer to room temperature for 20-30 minutes before serving, to soften slightly. Serve with fresh fruit, such as strawberries, raspberries or fresh fruit salad.

Variations: Use brandy or a liqueur in place of the whiskey. Substitute other dried fruit, such as chopped apricots, sultanas or glacé cherries in place of the raisins, and other chopped nuts, such as brazil nuts, hazelnuts or almonds in place of the walnuts.

CARAMEL CREAM

Serves 4-6

115 g/4 ½ oz sugar
600 ml/1 pint milk

4 eggs
few drops of vanilla essence

METHOD

1 Put 100 g/4 oz sugar in a heavy-based pan with 150 ml/5 fl oz water and heat until the sugar has dissolved. Continue heating, without stirring, until it is a golden brown colour. Remove from the heat before it darkens too much or it will taste bitter. Pour it into a warmed 15 cm/6 in soufflé dish, rotating the dish so all the base is coated. Leave to set. Meanwhile, preheat the oven to 170°C/325°F/GAS MARK 3.

2 Warm the milk. Beat the eggs with the remaining sugar and pour the milk over them. Whisk in the vanilla essence. Strain the custard into the dish.

3 Stand the dish in a roasting pan containing enough hot water to come halfway up the sides and bake for about 1 hour, until just set and firm to touch.

4 Turn out very carefully onto a warm dish and serve hot or cold, with cream if wished.

Variation: Make the caramel cream in individual ramekins or moulds and bake for 40 minutes.

PAVLOVA

Serves 6

3 egg whites
175 g/6 oz caster sugar
2.5 ml/½ tsp vanilla essence
2.5 ml1/2 tsp white wine vinegar

5 ml/1 tsp cornflour
300 ml/10 fl oz double cream
350 g/12 oz fresh fruit (raspberries, strawberries, blueberries)

METHOD

1 Preheat the oven to 150°C/300°F/GAS MARK 2. Draw an 18 cm/7 in circle on a sheet of non-stick and place the paper marked side down on a baking sheet.

2 Whisk the egg whites in a large bowl until stiff.

3 Whisk in half the sugar, then fold in the remaining sugar with the vanilla essence, vinegar and cornflour.

4 Spread the meringue over the circle and bake for about 1 hour, until crisp and dry. Transfer to a wire rack to cool, then peel off the paper.

5 Whip the cream until stiff. Place the meringue on a flat serving plate, spoon the cream on it and arrange the fruit on top. Serve immediately.

STRAWBERRY SHORTCAKE

Serves 6

For the shortcake:

225 g/8 oz butter or margarine, softened
100 g/4 oz caster sugar

225 g/8 oz plain flour
100 g/4 oz cornflour or ground rice

For the filling:

225 g/8 oz strawberries
150 ml/5 fl oz whipping cream
caster sugar for dusting

METHOD

1 Preheat the oven 170°C/325°F/GAS MARK 3. Grease two 18 cm/7 in sandwich tins.
2 Cream the butter and sugar until light and fluffy. Sift the flour and cornflour or ground rice and mix well, then knead to form a soft dough.
3 Press the mixture into the tins and bake for 30-35 minutes, until golden brown. Leave to cool in the tins for 10 minutes, then remove from the tins and cool on a wire rack.
4 Slice half the strawberries and lightly crush the remainder with a fork. Whip the cream with sugar to taste. Stir the crushed strawberries into the cream.
5 Spoon half the cream mixture over one shortcake, arrange the strawberry slices on top and spoon the remaining cream over the top. Carefully place the other shortcake on top and dredge with caster sugar. Serve cut into wedges.

LEMON DATE TARTLETS

Makes 12

175 g/6 oz ready-made shortcrust pastry
milk or beaten egg, to glaze

For the filling:

25 g/1 oz butter or margarine
175 g/6 oz dates, chopped
25 g/1 oz caster sugar

juice of ½ a lemon
2.5 ml/½ tsp finely grated lemon zest
1 egg, beaten

METHOD

1 Preheat the oven to 200°C/400°F/GAS MARK 6.
2 On a lightly floured surface, roll out the pastry and use to line a tartlet tin. Reserve the trimmings.
3 Melt the butter and add the dates, sugar, lemon juice and zest, and the beaten egg. Mix well and cook over a low heat for a few minutes, stirring continuously, until the mixture thickens.
4 Place a spoonful of the mixture in each pastry case. Roll out the pastry trimmings and cut them into thin strips. Place them over the filling. Brush the pastry strips with milk or beaten egg to glaze.
5 Bake for 15-20 minutes, until light golden brown. Transfer to a wire rack to cool. Serve warm or cold with cream or ice cream.

MINCEMEAT AND APPLE PIES

Makes about 20

1 quantity rough puff pastry (see Cheesy celery rolls, page 34)
milk, to glaze

For the filling:

100 g/4 oz cooking apple (peeled weight)
300 g/10 oz mincemeat
15 ml/1 tbsp brandy (optional)

finely grated zest of 1 small lemon
2.5 ml/½ tsp mixed spice (optional)
icing sugar for dusting

METHOD

1 Preheat the oven to 230°C/450°F/GAS MARK 8.
2 Grate the cooking apple and mix it with the mincemeat, brandy, if using, and the lemon zest. Add the mixed spice, if using.
3 On a lightly floured surface, roll out the pastry to about 3 mm/⅛ in thickness. Cut out about 20 rounds with a 7.5 cm/3 in fluted cutter and the same number of rounds with a 5.5 cm /2 ¼ in cutter.
4 Line tartlet tins with the larger rounds and fill with the fruit mixture. Dampen the edges and cover with the pastry lids. Brush with milk and bake for 20-25 minutes, until light golden brown. Dust with icing sugar to serve.

BUTTERSCOTCH PIE

Serves 4-6

175 g/6 oz ready-made shortcrust pastry
100 g/4 oz soft brown sugar
100 g/4 oz butter
45 ml/3 tbsp golden syrup

45 ml/3 tbsp milk
few drops of vanilla essence
2 eggs, separated
75 g/3 oz caster sugar

METHOD

1 Preheat the oven 200°C/400°F/GAS MARK 6.
2 On a lightly floured surface, roll out the pastry and use to line a 20 cm/8 in flan tin. Chill for 15 minutes. Bake blind for 10-15 minutes. Remove the paper and baking beans and bake for another 10-15 minutes, until firm and pale golden.
3 Reduce the oven temperature to 150°C/300°F/GAS MARK 2.
4 Put the brown sugar, butter, golden syrup, milk and vanilla essence in a heatproof bowl set over a pan of gently simmering water and stir until blended. Add the egg yolks and beat well. Pour the mixture into the baked pastry case.
5 Whisk the egg whites in a large bowl until stiff. Whisk in half the sugar, then fold in the remaining sugar.
6 Spoon or pipe the meringue on top of the filling. Bake for about 30-35 minutes, until the meringue is set and golden brown. Serve hot or cold, with whipped cream.

Note: Thickening the butterscotch filling with egg yolks gives the centre of the pie an attractive layered effect when it is cooked and sliced.

RHUBARB FLAN
Serves 4-6

For the pastry:

200 g/7 oz plain flour
pinch of salt
90 g/3 ½ oz butter or margarine

5 ml/1 tsp caster sugar
1 small egg, beaten

For the filling:
450 g/1 lb rhubarb, washed and cut into 4 cm/1 ½ in pieces
100 g/4 oz caster sugar
30 ml/2 tbsp cornflour

METHOD
1 Preheat the oven to 200°C/400°F/GAS MARK 6.
2 Place the flour and salt in a bowl and rub in the butter until the mixture resembles breadcrumbs. Add the sugar. Stir in the beaten egg and enough water to make a firm, smooth dough.
3 On a lightly floured surface, roll out the pastry and use to line a 23 cm/9 in flan tin. Chill for 15 minutes. Bake blind for 10-15 minutes. Remove the paper and baking beans and bake for another 15-20 minutes, until firm and pale golden.
4 Place the rhubarb in a pan with 150 ml/5 fl oz water and simmer gently until soft but not stringy. Add the sugar and stir until dissolved.
5 Blend the cornflour with a little water, stir it into the rhubarb. Bring to the boil, stirring continuously until the mixture thickens. Reduce the heat and simmer for 3 minutes.
6 Pour the rhubarb into the flan case and leave to cool. Serve cool or chilled with cream, ice cream or custard.

LEMON MERINGUE PIE
Serves 4-6

175 g/6 oz ready-made shortcrust pastry
finely grated zest and juice of 2 lemons
50-75 g/2-3 oz granulated sugar

75 ml/5 tbsp cornflour
2 eggs, separated
75 g/3 oz caster sugar

METHOD
1 Preheat the oven 200°C/400°F/GAS MARK 6.
2 On a lightly floured surface, roll out the pastry and use to line a 20 cm/8 in flan tin. Chill for 15 minutes. Bake blind for 10-15 minutes. Remove the paper and baking beans and bake for another 10-15 minutes, until firm and pale golden. Reduce the oven temperature to 150°C/300°F/GAS MARK 2.
3 Put the lemon zest and juice, granulated sugar and 300 ml/10 fl oz water in a pan. Heat gently until the sugar has dissolved.
4 Mix the cornflour to a smooth paste with 90 ml/6 tbsp water and stir it into the lemon mixture. Bring to the boil, stirring continuously, and cook for 1 minute, until thickened. Leave to cool slightly, then stir in the egg yolks.
5 Whisk the egg whites in a large bowl until stiff. Whisk in half the sugar, then fold in the remaining sugar.
6 Pour the lemon filling into the pastry case and level the surface. Pile the meringue on top of the filling and swirl it with a palette knife. Bake for 30-35 minutes, until the meringue is set and golden brown.

Rhubarb Flan
Lemon Meringue Pie

CAKES AND BISCUITS

'Mum baked so much she often ended up giving half of it away – no wonder she was so popular with the neighbours.'

The cakes in this chapter are all guaranteed to bring back nostalgic memories. They include May Hunniford's prize-winning Madeira cake, Irish whiskey cake and chocolate sandwich cake, as well as tea time favourites such as coffee kisses, coconut buns and melting moments – so named because they disappeared in moments as they came out of the oven – dainty sherry rolls and chocolate raisin crunchies made for special occasion teas.

COFFEE CAKE

75 g/3 oz butter or margarine
50 g/2 oz caster sugar
30 ml/2 tbsp golden syrup
2 eggs, beaten

175 g/6 oz plain flour
5 ml/1 tsp baking powder
10 ml/2 tsp coffee essence
45-60 ml/3-4 tbsp buttermilk, to mix

For the buttercream filling and topping:

175 g/6 oz icing sugar
75 g/3 oz butter
10 ml/2 tsp coffee essence

a little milk, to mix
icing sugar for dusting

METHOD

1 Preheat the oven to 180°C/350°F/GAS MARK 4. Grease two 18 cm/7 in sandwich tins (alternatively, use two fluted flan tins).

2 Cream the butter, sugar and syrup. Beat in half the beaten egg with the flour and baking powder, then beat in the rest of the egg.

3 Add the coffee essence and enough buttermilk to beat to a soft dropping consistency. Pour the mixture into the tins and level the surface. Bake for 20-25 minutes, until risen and firm to the touch. Cool on a wire rack.

4 To make the buttercream, beat together the 175 g/6 oz icing sugar, butter, coffee essence and enough milk to make it spreadable. Sandwich the cakes together with half the buttercream and pipe the rest around the top edge of the cake. Dust the centre with icing sugar.

Variations: Omit the coffee essence and add 15 ml/1 tbsp cocoa powder to the mixture, or the finely grated rind of 1 lemon or 1 orange.

IRISH WHISKEY CAKE

350 g/12 oz mixed dried fruit
60 ml/4 tbsp whiskey
175 g/6 oz butter
175 g/6 oz soft brown sugar
grated zest of 1 orange
3 eggs, beaten

225 g/8 oz plain flour
5 ml/1 tsp baking powder
pinch of salt
5 ml/1 tsp mixed spice
50 g/2 oz ground almonds

METHOD

1 Soak the mixed fruit in the whiskey overnight.

2 Preheat the oven to 170°C/325°f/GAS MARK 3. Grease and base line a 20 cm/8 in cake tin.

3 Cream the butter and sugar until fluffy. Add the orange zest. Gradually beat in the eggs.

4 Sift the flour, baking powder, salt and mixed spice and add to the egg mixture with the fruit and whiskey and the ground almonds.

5 Turn the mixture into the cake tin and bake for 1 ½-2 hours.

Variation: Cover the top of the mixture with halved glacé cherries and sprinkle with demerara sugar before baking, to give an attractive crunchy topping.

Coffee cake
Irish Whiskey cake

MADEIRA CAKE

175 g/6 oz butter, softened
175 g/6 oz caster sugar
finely grated zest of 1 lemon
3 eggs, beaten
225 g/8 oz plain flour
10 ml/2 tsp baking powder

pinch of salt
pinch of ground cinnamon
30 ml/2 tbsp milk
10 ml/2 tsp lemon juice
2-3 thin slices citron peel (optional)

METHOD

1 Preheat the oven to 170°C/325°F/GAS MARK 3. Grease and line an 18 cm/7 in round cake tin.

2 Cream the butter and sugar together in a bowl until light and fluffy, then beat in the lemon zest.

3 Add the eggs, a little at a time, beating well after each addition, sifting in a little of the flour, if necessary, to prevent curdling.

4 Sift the flour with the baking powder, salt and cinnamon, and lightly stir it into the creamed mixture with the milk and lemon juice — it is most important not to beat at this stage, just mix all the ingredients thoroughly.

5 Pour the mixture into the tin, smooth the top and place the citron peel, if using, in the centre. Bake for 1 ½-1 ¾ hours, until a fine skewer inserted into the centre comes out clean. Cool on a wire rack.

CHOCOLATE SANDWICH CAKE

100 g/2 oz butter or margarine
100 g/4 oz caster sugar
60 ml/4 tbsp golden syrup
20 ml/4 tsp cocoa powder

10 ml/2 tsp bicarbonate of soda
10 ml/2 tsp baking powder
225 g/8 oz plain flour
300 ml/10 fl oz buttermilk

For the filling:

100 g/4 oz icing sugar
50 g/2 oz butter, softened

few drops of vanilla essence (optional)
15-30 ml/1-2 tbsp milk

For the icing:

100 g/4 oz icing sugar
10 ml/2 tsp cocoa powder, plus extra for sprinkling
15 ml/1 tbsp hot water

METHOD

1 Preheat the oven to 180°C/350°F/GAS MARK 4. Grease and line two 18 cm/7 in sandwich tins.

2 To make the cake, put all the ingredients except the flour and buttermilk into a pan and heat gently until the butter and syrup have melted. Sift the flour and fold into the melted mixture.

3 Make a well in the centre and add the buttermilk all at once and beat well to a fairly thick batter. Pour into the tins and bake for 25-30 minutes, until firm to the touch.

4 To make the filling, beat together the icing sugar, butter, vanilla essence, if using, and enough milk to make it spreadable. Sandwich the cakes together with the filling.

5 To make the icing, sift the icing sugar into a bowl. Dissolve the 10 ml/2 tsp cocoa powder in the hot water and stir it into the icing sugar. The icing should be thick enough to coat the back of a spoon. Spread the icing over the top of the cake, then sprinkle cocoa powder over it.

Chocolate Sandwich Cake

SULTANA CAKE

225 g/8 oz butter or margarine
225 g/8 oz soft brown sugar
4 eggs, beaten
325 g/11 oz plain flour
5 ml/1 tsp baking powder
350 g/12 oz sultanas

350 g/12 oz raisins
100 g/4 oz glacé cherries
25 g/1 oz ground almonds
zest and juice of ½ an orange
zest and juice of ½ a lemon

METHOD

1 Preheat the oven to 160°C/325°F/GAS MARK 2. Grease and base line a 23 cm/9 in cake tin.
2 Cream the butter and sugar until fluffy. Add the eggs, a little at a time, beating well after each addition.
3 Sift the flour and baking powder together, then fold into the creamed mixture. Stir in the fruit, almonds and the orange and lemon zest and juice.
4 Turn the mixture in to the tin and bake for about 1 ¾-2 hours. Cover with a sheet of greaseproof paper if the cake is browning too fast.

APPLE GINGERBREAD WITH CINNAMON ICING

225 g/8 oz cooking apples, peeled,
  cored and sliced (peeled weight)
75 g/3 oz butter
175 g/6 oz golden syrup
100 g/4 oz soft brown sugar
150 ml/5 fl oz milk
1 egg, beaten

225 g/8 oz plain flour
pinch of salt
10 ml/2 tsp ground ginger
5 ml/1 tsp ground mixed spice
5 ml/1 tsp baking powder
5 ml/1 tsp bicarbonate of soda

For the icing:
100 g/4 oz icing sugar
2.5-5 ml/½-1 tsp ground cinnamon

METHOD

1 Preheat the oven to 170°C/325°F/GAS MARK 3. Grease and line a 20 cm/8 in round or an 18-20 cm/7-8 in square cake tin.
2 Put the apples in a pan with 15 ml/1 tbsp water and cook until soft and mushy. Allow to cool slightly. Put the butter, syrup and sugar in a separate pan and warm gently over low heat until melted and well blended. Cool slightly, then beat in the milk and egg.
3 Sift the dry ingredients into a bowl, add the syrup mixture and beat well. Add the stewed apple and beat until well mixed.
4 Pour the mixture into the tin and bake for 1 ¼-1 ½ hours, until firm to the touch. Turn out of the tin and leave to cool on a wire rack.
5 To make the icing, sift the sugar and cinnamon into a bowl and gradually add 15 ml/1 tbsp warm water. The icing should be thick enough to coat the back of a spoon. Pour the icing over the cake and serve cut into slices or squares.

Note: This makes a heavier gingerbread than the traditional version made without apple. Omit the apple, if preferred.

Apple Gingerbread with Cinnamon Icing

STEAMED DATE LOAF

175 g/6 oz butter
175 g/6 oz dark soft brown sugar
175 g/6 oz plain flour
3 eggs
15 ml/1 tbsp sherry or orange juice
2.5 ml/½ tsp baking powder
2.5 ml/½ tsp mixed spice
freshly grated nutmeg
225 g/8 oz currants
225 g/8 oz sultanas
50 g/2 oz shredded almonds
almond halves, to decorate

METHOD

1 Preheat the oven to 150°C/300°F/GAS MARK 2. Grease and base-line an 18 cm/7 in round cake tin.

2 Cream the butter and sugar together in a bowl until light and fluffy.

3 Add the eggs, a little at a time, beating well after each addition. Stir in the sherry or orange juice.

4 Sift the flour with the baking powder, mixed spice and nutmeg. Mix the currants, sultanas and almonds together and stir 15 ml/1 tbsp flour into them.

5 Lightly stir the flour into the creamed mixture and then stir in the dried fruit.

6 Pour the mixture into the tin, smooth the top and then decorate with the almond halves. Bake for 2 ¼-2 ½ hours. Leave to cool in the tin for 20 minutes, then turn out and finish cooling on a wire rack.

BOILED CAKE

225 g/8 oz sultanas
225 g/8 oz raisins or currants
50 g/2 oz glacé cherries
50 g/2 oz mixed peel
175 g/6 oz butter
100 g/4 oz soft brown sugar
225 g/8 oz plain flour
5 ml/1 tsp bicarbonate of soda
2.5 ml/½ tsp ground ginger
3 eggs, beaten

METHOD

1 Preheat the oven to 180°C/350°F/GAS MARK 4. Grease and line a 20 cm/8 in round cake tin.

2 Put all the fruit and mixed peel into a pan and add the butter, sugar and 175 ml/6 fl oz water. Bring to the boil, then boil gently for 5 minutes, stirring frequently. Remove from the heat and cool slightly.

3 Sift the flour, bicarbonate of soda and ginger into a bowl. Pour in the boiled mixture and mix well. Add the eggs and beat well.

4 Pour the mixture into the cake tin and bake for 1 ¼ hours. Leave to cool slightly in the tin, then turn out and cool completely on a wire rack.

Boiled cake

SIMNEL CAKE

175 g/6 oz butter or margarine
175 g/6 oz caster sugar
grated zest of 1 lemon
2 eggs
175 g/6 oz plain flour
175 g/6 oz currants and sultanas
50 g/2 oz mixed peel
450 g/1 lb marzipan

METHOD

1 Preheat the oven to 170°C/325°F/GAS MARK 3. Grease and line an 18 cm/7 in round cake tin. Grease the greaseproof paper.
2 Cream the butter, sugar and lemon zest until pale and fluffy. Beat in the eggs, one at a time.
3 Sift the flour and fold it into the mixture with a metal spoon. Add the fruit and mixed peel. Mix together to a soft dropping consistency.
4 Roll out 175 g/6 oz of the marzipan and shape into a round the same diameter as the cake tin.
5 Spoon half the cake mixture into the cake tin, place the round of marzipan on top, then spoon the rest of the cake mixture over it.
6 Bake for 2-2 ½ hours, then leave the cake to cool. Roll out 150 g/5 oz of the remaining marzipan to a round the same size as the cake and place it on the cake. Roll the remaining marzipan into 11 balls and place them around the top edge of the cake.

Note: Simnel cake was traditionally made as a Mothering Sunday gift. Each year on the fourth Sunday in Lent, servant girls were allowed to have a day off to visit their mothers. Their mistress allowed them to bake a cake to take home, and it was usually a simnel cake. The name came from the Latin *simila*, meaning fine wheat flour.

Nowadays, simnel cake is still a festive cake, served on Easter Sunday. The balls of marzipan on the top of the cake represent the 11 faithful disciples.

HUNNIFORD CHRISTMAS CAKE

450 g/1 lb raisins
450 g/1 lb sultanas
175 g/6 oz glacé cherries
400 g/14 oz plain flour
1.25 ml/¼ tsp mixed spice
pinch of salt
300 g/10 oz butter
300 g/10 oz soft brown sugar

grated zest of orange
grated zest of 1 lemon
5-6 eggs, beaten
75 g/3 oz ground almonds
30 ml/2 tbsp brandy
100 g/4 oz apricot jam
800 g/1 ¾ lb marzipan

For the icing:

4 egg whites
900 g/2 lb icing sugar

15 ml/1 tbsp lemon juice
10 ml/2 tsp glycerine

METHOD

1 Wash and dry all the fruit the day before you make the cake.

2 The next day, preheat the oven to 170°C/300°F/GAS MARK 3. Grease and line a 20 cm/8 in square cake tin, using a double thickness of greaseproof paper. Tie a band of double-thickness greaseproof paper round the outside of the tin.

3 Sift the flour and mixed spice into a bowl with the salt.

4 In a separate bowl, cream the butter, sugar and orange and lemon zest until light and fluffy. Add the beaten eggs gradually, beating well.

5 Gradually fold the flour lightly into the mixture with a metal spoon, then fold in the ground almonds. Finally fold in the fruit.

6 Turn the mixture into the tin, spreading it evenly, and make a hollow in the centre.

7 Bake for 1 hour, then reduce the oven temperature to 130°C/250°F/GAS MARK 1 and bake for a further 3 hours.

8 Leave the cake to cool, then remove the lining paper, prick the bottom of the cake with a fork or a fine skewer and pour the brandy into the cake.

9 Put the apricot jam in a pan with 30 ml/2 tbsp water and heat gently until the jam melts. Bring it to the boil and simmer for 1 minute, then rub it through a sieve. Brush the warm jam over the sides of the cake.

10 On a surface dusted with icing sugar, roll out two thirds of the marzipan and use it to cover the sides of the cake (*see* **Note**). Smooth the joins with a palette knife and trim the top and bottom edges so they are square. Brush the top of the cake with the jam (reheating it, if necessary). Roll out the remaining marzipan and use to cover the top of the cake. Leave it to dry for 4-5 days before icing the cake.

TO DECORATE

1 To make the icing, whisk the egg whites in a bowl until frothy, then sift in one quarter of the icing sugar, stirring with a wooden spoon. Gradually add more of the sugar, beating well after each addition, until about three quarters of the sugar is added.

2 Add the lemon juice and beat until the icing is smooth, then beat in the rest of the icing sugar. Stir in the glycerine. Cover and leave for 24 hours before icing the cake.

3 Spread two thirds of the icing on the top and sides of the cake, using a palette knife. Leave the first layer of icing for 24 hours.

4 Spoon the remaining icing on the top of the previous layer, then pull the icing into peaks, using a palette knife or the back of a teaspoon. Leave to dry for 24 hours.

Note: If you want a perfect cake, Lena's advice is to '*Give it a kiss before it goes into the oven*'.
For a foolproof way to cover the cake with marzipan, measure around the cake with a piece of string. Roll out two thirds of the marzipan to a rectangle half the length of the string and twice the depth of the cake, then cut the rectangle in half lengthwise. Lift each piece and place in position round the cake. Smooth the joins and roll the marzipan with a jam jar to secure it firmly in position. Roll out the remaining marzipan to a square the same size as the top of the cake, then lift it onto the cake with the rolling pin. Roll gently with the rolling pin to stick it to the glaze.

DOUGHNUTS

225 g/8 oz plain flour
pinch of salt
25 g/1 oz butter or margarine
15 g/½ oz fresh yeast
25 g/1 oz sugar

150 ml/5 fl oz milk
2 egg yolks
vegetable oil for deep frying
caster sugar and ground cinnamon,
    mixed together

METHOD

1 Grease a baking sheet. Warm the flour and add the salt. Rub the butter into the flour.

2 In a separate bowl, cream the yeast with 5 ml/1 tsp of the sugar. Warm the milk and pour it over the egg yolks in a bowl, then add to the yeast.

3 Add the yeast mixture to the flour and mix to a light dough using your hand. Beat for 10 minutes, until the mixture leaves your hand clean.

4 Flour the bottom of the bowl and leave the dough to rise in a warm place, such as an airing cupboard, covered with oiled clingfilm, until doubled in size.

5 Turn out the dough on to a floured surface and knead well until free from cracks, then roll out to about 12 mm/½ in thick. Cut into large circles and cut out the centres. Place them on the greased baking sheet and leave to rise again in a warm place for 10 minutes.

6 Heat the oil until faintly smoking, then fry the doughnuts, a few at a time, for 6-8 minutes, until browned. Drain the doughnuts on absorbent kitchen paper, then toss in the sugar and cinnamon mixture.

CURD AND JAM SLICES

Makes 12-16

75 g/3 oz butter or margarine
50 g/2 oz caster sugar
175 g/6 oz plain flour

1 egg, beaten
jam or lemon curd for filling

METHOD

1 Preheat the oven to 190°C/375°F/GAS MARK 5.

2 Cream the butter and sugar together in a bowl. Gradually work in the flour, using enough beaten egg to make a stiff paste. Turn on to a floured surface and knead well.

3 Roll out to an oblong 15 cm/6 in wide and 6 mm/¼ in thick. Divide in half lengthwise, spread one half with jam or lemon curd, keeping the edges clear. Place the other piece of dough on top and pinch the edges to secure them.

4 Brush with beaten egg and lightly mark into fingers with a sharp knife. Bake for 30 minutes, until golden brown. Carefully cut into fingers and transfer to a wire rack to cool.

Variation: To make pinwheel biscuits, roll out the dough but do not cut it in half. Spread jam or lemon curd over the dough, then roll up the dough from one long side like a swiss roll. Chill the dough in the freezer for 30 minutes, then cut the roll into slices. Place on a baking sheet and bake as above.

Curd and Jam Pinwheels

COFFEE KISSES

Makes 9

175 g/6 oz self-raising flour
75 g/3 oz butter or margarine
75 g/3 oz sugar
1 egg, beaten
5 ml/1 tsp coffee essence

For the icing:
50 g/2 oz butter
100 g/4 oz icing sugar
10 ml/2 tsp coffee essence

METHOD

1 Preheat the oven to 190°C/375°F/GAS MARK 5. Grease a baking sheet.
2 Sift the flour into a bowl and rub in the butter until the mixture resembles breadcrumbs. Stir in the sugar. Mix in the egg and coffee essence.
3 Roll the mixture into balls and place on the baking sheet, or place teaspoonfuls of mixture on the baking sheet. Bake for 20 minutes, until lightly browned.
4 To make the icing, cream the butter until soft. Sift the icing sugar and gradually beat it in. Stir in the coffee essence and a little warm water, if necessary.
5 When the coffee kisses are cold, sandwich them together with the icing.

COCONUT BUNS

Makes 22

250 g/9 oz ready-made shortcrust pastry
60 ml/4 tbsp raspberry jam
2 egg whites
100 g/4 oz caster sugar
100 g/4 oz desiccated coconut
glacé cherries, quartered, to decorate (optional)

METHOD

1 Preheat the oven to 180°C/350°F/GAS MARK 4.
2 On a floured surface, roll out the pastry fairly thinly. Using a 6 cm/2 ½ in plain or fluted cutter, cut out rounds and use to line tartlet tins, re-rolling the trimmings to make 22 rounds. Place about 2.5 ml/½ tsp jam in each one.
3 Whisk the egg whites until stiff, fold in the sugar and whisk again until stiff. Lightly mix in the coconut. Spoon about a heaped teaspoonful of the mixture into each tartlet case to cover the jam. Top each one with a quartered glacé cherry, if using. Bake for 15 minutes until lightly coloured and crisp. Leave the buns to cool on a wire rack before serving.

Coconut Buns
Coffee Kisses

SURPRISE FAIRY CAKES

Makes 12

75 g/3 oz butter or margarine
75 g/3 oz caster sugar
2 eggs, beaten
175 g/6 oz plain flour
5 ml/1 tsp baking powder
pinch of salt
few drops of vanilla essence
45-60 ml/3-4 tbsp milk
100 g/4 oz mincemeat
icing sugar for dusting

METHOD

1 Preheat the oven to 200°C/400°F/GAS MARK 6. Grease a 12-hole tartlet tin or line the holes with paper cake cases.
2 Cream the butter and sugar in a bowl. Gradually beat in the eggs. Fold in the flour, baking powder and salt. Stir in the vanilla essence. Add enough milk to make a soft dropping consistency.
3 Place a little cake mixture in each tartlet tin or paper case. Place a small amount of mincemeat on top and cover with a little more cake mixture. Bake for 20-25 minutes, until golden.
4 Turn out and cool on a wire rack. Dust with icing sugar just before serving.

Variation: Use jam, lemon curd or marmalade instead of the mincemeat.

MELTING MOMENTS

Makes about 10

75 g/3 oz butter or margarine
25 g/1 oz caster sugar
150 g/5 oz plain flour
a little milk
few drops of vanilla essence

For the filling:
50 g/2 oz butter, softened
100 g/4 oz icing sugar
about 15 ml/1 tbsp milk

METHOD

1 Preheat the oven to 190°C/375°F/GAS MARK 5. Grease a baking sheet.
2 Beat the butter and sugar until very soft and creamy, then gradually beat in the flour, adding a little milk if the mixture becomes too stiff. Add the vanilla essence.
3 Place spoonfuls of the mixture onto the baking sheet and bake for about 20 minutes.
4 To make the filling, cream the butter in a bowl, then sift and beat in the icing sugar, adding just enough milk to make it soft enough to spread.
5 Leave the biscuits to cool, then sandwich together with the filling.

SHAH BISCUITS

Makes 12-16

50 g/2 oz butter or margarine
50 g/2 oz caster sugar
15 ml/1 tbsp golden syrup
½ an egg
100 g/4 oz plain flour
2.5 ml/½ tsp ground ginger

METHOD

1 Preheat the oven to 180°C/350°F/GAS MARK 4.
2 Cream the butter and sugar, then beat in the syrup and egg.
3 Gradually work in the flour and ground ginger, turning the mixture onto a board and kneading it lightly, if necessary.
4 Shape the dough into a long roll and cut it into slices about 12 mm/½ in thick, then shape them into balls. Place them on the baking sheets leaving plenty of space between them. Leave to stand for a few minutes, then bake for 15-20 minutes.

Variation: Place a small piece of blanched almond on each biscuit before baking.

CHOCOLATE BISCUITS

Makes about 16

100 g/4 oz butter
50 g/2 oz caster sugar
100 g/4 oz self-raising flour
75 g/3 oz desiccated coconut
10 ml/2 tsp cocoa powder
100-175 g/4-6 oz plain chocolate
50 g/2 oz white chocolate

METHOD

1 Preheat the oven to 170°C/325°F/GAS MARK 3. Grease a 23 cm/9 in square tin.
2 Cream the butter and sugar in a bowl. Add the flour, coconut and cocoa powder and mix well.
3 Spread the mixture in the tin and bake for 20 minutes. Allow to cool slightly before cutting into squares or bars.
4 Melt the plain and white chocolate in separate pans. Spread the plain chocolate over the biscuits. Drizzle the white chocolate over the top and draw a skewer through it to give a feathered effect.

Variation: If you do not want to be bothered with the feathered effect, omit the white chocolate and simply spread the plain chocolate over the biscuits.

WONDER BITES

Makes about 20

50 g/2 oz butter
100 g/4 oz icing sugar, sifted
5 ml/1 tsp coffee essence
75 g/3 oz desiccated coconut

50 g/2 oz chopped mixed nuts
75 g/3 oz glacé cherries, chopped finely
225 g/8 oz plain chocolate
cocoa powder for dusting

METHOD
1 Cream the butter and sugar in a bowl until pale and fluffy. Add all the remaining ingredients, except the chocolate, and mix well.
2 Roll the mixture into small balls and set aside until firm.
3 Melt the chocolate in a heatproof bowl set over a pan of simmering water. Coat the balls in chocolate and place on greaseproof paper to dry, then dust with cocoa powder.

SNOWBALLS

Makes 16-18

100 g/4 oz butter or margarine
100 g/2 oz sugar
5 ml/1 tsp golden syrup
20 ml/4 tsp drinking chocolate powder

100 g/4 oz digestive biscuit crumbs
100 g/4 oz desiccated coconut
extra desiccated coconut for coating

METHOD
1 Heat the butter, sugar and syrup in a pan until the sugar has melted.
2 Remove from the heat and stir in the drinking chocolate powder, biscuit crumbs and coconut.
3 Roll the mixture into balls. Spread out the coconut for coating on a plate and roll the balls in the coconut until coated.

CHOCOLATE RAISIN CRUNCHIES

Makes 20

350 g/12 oz plain or milk chocolate
350 g/12 oz raisins

50 g/2 oz cornflakes
50 g/2 oz blanched almonds, sliced

METHOD
1 Place 20 paper cake cases in tartlet tins.
2 Melt the chocolate in a heatproof bowl set over a pan of simmering water. Remove the bowl from the heat and stir in all the remaining ingredients until well mixed.
3 Place spoonfuls of the mixture into the paper cases and leave to set.

Chocolate Raisin Crunchies
Snowballs
Wonder bites

PEANUT CRUNCH
Makes 24

25 g/1 oz butter
225 g/8 oz peanut butter
150 g/5 oz icing sugar

100 g/4 oz rice krispies
175 g/6 oz plain chocolate

METHOD

1 Melt the butter and peanut butter in a pan. Stir in the icing sugar, then add the rice krispies and mix well.
2 Spread the mixture in a swiss roll tin, pressing to level the surface.
3 Melt the chocolate in a heatproof bowl set over a pan of simmering water and pour it over the peanut mixture. Leave to set in the refrigerator, then cut into squares.

DATE AND RAISIN BALLS
Makes about 24

175 g/6 oz stoned dates
175 g/6 oz raisins
5 ml/1 tsp grated orange zest

pinch of ground cinnamon
few drops of vanilla essence
225 g/8 oz plain chocolate

METHOD

1 Chop the dates and raisins finely, or put them through a mincer. Add the orange zest, cinnamon and vanilla essence, and mix well. Form the mixture into small balls.
2 Melt the chocolate in a heatproof bowl set over a pan of simmering water. Dip the balls into the melted chocolate, one at a time. Place them on oiled greaseproof paper and leave to set.

CHERRY, WALNUT AND MARSHMALLOW BITES
Makes about 16

350 g/12 oz glacé cherries, finely chopped
25 g/1 oz chopped walnuts
25 g/1 oz icing sugar

4 pink and 4 white marshmallows, cut into small pieces
60-75 ml/4-5 tbsp evaporated milk
175 g/6 oz desiccated coconut

METHOD

1 Put the cherries, walnuts and sugar in a bowl. Cut the marshmallows into small pieces, using damp scissors to prevent them sticking, and add them to the bowl.
2 Add the milk and coconut, and mix well.
3 Place spoonfuls of the mixture into paper cases (or use petit fours cases, in which case you will need about 30) and leave to set in the refrigerator.

SHERRY ROLLS

Makes about 12

75 g/3 oz shortbread biscuits
75 g/3 oz ground almonds
10 ml/2 tsp caster sugar
20 ml/4 tsp sherry
about 30 ml/2 tbsp hot milk
100 g/4 oz plain chocolate
vermicelli for coating

METHOD

1 Put the shortbread biscuits in a plastic bag and crush them with a rolling pin. Add the ground almonds, caster sugar and sherry, and mix well.
2 Stir in enough hot milk to make a sticky mixture. Shape into small rolls and leave to cool.
3 Melt the chocolate in a heatproof bowl set over a pan of simmering water. Dip the rolls in the chocolate, then roll them in the vermicelli. Leave to set.

CHOCOLATE FANCIES

Makes about 22

50 g/2 oz butter or margarine
100 g/4 oz caster sugar
30 ml/2 tbsp milk
50 g/2 oz chopped walnuts
15 ml/1 tbsp cocoa powder
15 ml/1 tbsp drinking chocolate powder
50 g/2 oz desiccated coconut
175 g/6 oz cake crumbs
175 g/6 oz plain chocolate
vermicelli for coating

METHOD

1 Put the butter, sugar and milk in a pan and bring to the boil.
2 Stir in the walnuts, cocoa powder, drinking chocolate powder, coconut and cake crumbs. Form the mixture into walnut-sized balls.
3 Melt the chocolate in a heatproof bowl set over a pan of simmering water. Dip the balls in the chocolate, then roll them in the vermicelli. Leave to set.

GINGER SNAPS

Makes about 22

225 g/8 oz plain flour
5 ml/1 tsp baking powder
pinch of mixed spice
5 ml/1 tsp ground ginger
50 g/2 oz butter or margarine
100 g/4 oz soft brown sugar
1 egg, beaten
30-45 ml/2-3 tbsp golden syrup

METHOD

1 Preheat the oven to 180°C/350°F/GAS MARK 4. Grease two baking sheets.
2 Sift the flour, baking powder and spices together. Rub in the butter until the mixture resembles bread crumbs. Stir in the sugar.
3 Add the beaten egg and syrup to make a soft consistency.
4 Take walnut-sized pieces of the mixture and roll them into balls. Place them well apart on the baking sheets. Bake for 15–20 minutes, until lightly browned.

OATMEAL BISCUITS

Makes about 10

75 g/3 oz butter or margarine
50 g/2 oz caster sugar
30 ml/2 tbsp golden syrup
1 egg, beaten
5 ml/1 tsp vanilla essence
100 g/4 oz fine oatmeal
175 g/6 oz plain flour
5 ml/1 tsp baking powder
2.5 ml/½ tsp bicarbonate of soda
pinch of salt

For the filling:
50 g/2 oz icing sugar
5 ml/1 tsp cocoa powder
25 g/1 oz butter or margarine

METHOD

1 Preheat the oven to 180°C/350°F/ GAS MARK 4. Grease a baking sheet.
2 Cream the butter, sugar and syrup. Add the egg and vanilla essence, then add the dry ingredients and mix well. Place small spoonfuls of mixture on the baking sheet and bake for 15-20 minutes, until lightly browned. Transfer to a wire rack to cool.
3 To make the filling, sift the icing sugar and cocoa powder into a bowl and mix in the butter until it forms a soft mixture, adding a little warm water, if necessary.
4 When the biscuits are cold, sandwich them together with the filling.

Ginger Snaps
Oatmeal Biscuits

PRESERVES

'There was always a pot of tea on the kitchen table, bread fresh from the oven and thick-spread jam made from fruit from the garden.'

Traditionally, whenever there was a glut of fresh fruit – strawberries in the garden, wild blackberries from the hedgerow – it would be turned into jam. Vegetables would be preserved for the winter in thick, chunky chutneys and pickles. Fruit cheeses are old-fashioned country fare, and the apple cheese in this chapter is a smooth, rich preserve that makes a delicious alternative to lemon curd.

APPLE CHEESE

450 g/1 lb cooking apples (peeled weight), roughly chopped
grated zest of 2 lemons
60 ml/4 tbsp lemon juice
225 g/8 oz sugar
75 g/3 oz butter
2 eggs, beaten

METHOD

1. Simmer the apples with the lemon zest and juice until the apples are tender, adding a little water if necessary to prevent the apples sticking and burning.
2. Remove from the heat and either sieve the pulp or beat it until smooth. Stir in the sugar and return the mixture to the heat. Bring to the boil and boil until thick.
3. Transfer the mixture to the top of a double boiler or a heatproof bowl set over a pan of gently simmering water (make sure the bottom of the bowl does not touch the water). Add the butter, stirring until it is melted. Add the beaten eggs and cook gently for 35-40 minutes.

Note: This recipe makes a refreshingly tart preserve which can be used as a filling for tarts, tartlets or cakes. It needs eating straight away: if you want a preserve for storing, increase the amount of sugar to 450 g/1 lb. Pot into jars and cover.

RHUBARB AND ORANGE JAM

1.4 kg/3 lb rhubarb
2 oranges
1.5 kg/3 ½ lb sugar

METHOD

1. Wash the rhubarb and cut it into chunks. Cut the orange into quarters. Cut up the pulp and mix it with the rhubarb. Mince the orange skin. Place it all in a bowl and leave to stand for 24 hours.
2. The next day, place it in a preserving pan. Bring to the boil and boil for 20-30 minutes. Meanwhile, prepare the jam jars as instructed on page 120. Once setting point is reached (*see* page 120) pot into jars and cover with jam pot covers in the usual way.

Note: This jam makes a delicious alternative to strawberry jam, spread on home-made scones covered with thick cream.

Preparing Preserve Jars

To prepare jars for jams and chutneys, wash jars (in the case of chutneys and pickles) and lids thoroughly in hot soapy water. Rinse well and stand upside-down to drain. Place a fairly thick wad of folded newspapers in the bottom of a roasting tin and place the jars, right side up, in the tin. Heat in a low oven until ready to use.

Testing for a Set

To test whether jam has reached setting point, remove the pan from the heat so the jam does not continue cooking while you are testing it. Place a small amount of jam on a cold plate or saucer, allow it to cool, then push a finger through it. If the surface of the jam wrinkles, the setting point of the jam has been reached.

Alternatively, dip a wooden spoon into the jam, let the jam cool slightly, then let it drop back into the pan. If setting point has been reached, the drops will run together forming flakes which break off sharply.

To test with a sugar thermometer, stir the jam and insert the thermometer in the middle of the pan. If the reading is 105°C/221°F, the jam should have reached setting point. The thermometer should be placed in hot water before and after testing the jam.

ROSEHIP JAM

700 g/1 ½ lb rosehips
1.4 kg/3 lb cooking apples, peeled and sliced
2-3 cloves
1.8 kg/4 lb sugar

METHOD

1 Put the rosehips in a preserving pan with 1.2 litres/2 pints water and bring slowly to the boil. Reduce the heat and simmer for 1 ½ hours.
2 Strain the juice through muslin or a sieve. Put the juice into a preserving pan, add the sliced apples and cloves, and simmer until the apples are soft.
3 Add the sugar and bring slowly to the boil. Boil for 20 minutes or until setting point is reached. Pot into jars and cover.

STRAWBERRY JAM

3.2 kg/7 lb strawberries
juice of 2 lemons
2.8 kg/6 lb sugar

METHOD
1 Put the strawberries and lemon juice in a preserving pan and heat gently, stirring constantly, for about 30 minutes, until reduced in volume.
2 Add the sugar, stir well, then bring to the boil and boil until setting point is reached.
3 Remove from the heat and remove the scum with a slotted spoon. Leave the jam to cool until a skin forms on the surface, then stir, pot into jars and cover.

DAMSON JAM

1.8 kg/4 lb sugar
175 ml/6 fl oz vinegar
175 ml/6 fl oz water
1.8 kg/4 lb ripe damsons

METHOD
1 Put the sugar, vinegar and water into a preserving pan. Bring to the boil and boil until syrupy. Add the fruit and boil for 10 minutes. Remove the stones and pot into jars and cover with vinegar-proof lids.

MARROW AND GINGER JAM

1.4 kg/3 lb peeled marrow
1.4 kg/3 lb sugar
rind and juice of 2 lemons
100 g/4 oz crystallised ginger, chopped

METHOD
1 Cut the marrow into cubes and put into a large bowl, sprinkling the layers with sugar. Leave to stand overnight.
2 The next day, transfer the marrow to a preserving pan. Tie the lemon rind in a piece of muslin and add to the pan with the ginger and lemon juice.
3 Bring to the boil and cook gently until the marrow is transparent and the syrup is thick. Remove the lemon rind, stir, then pot into jars and cover.

Note: Adding 15 ml/1 tbsp golden syrup at the end prevents crystallising.

BRAMBLE JELLY

450 g/1 lb blackberries
1 medium-sized cooking apple, peeled and chopped
sugar

METHOD

1 Put the blackberries and apple into a pan with 75 ml/3 fl oz water and simmer until the fruit is soft.
2 Spoon the fruit into a jelly bag and leave to strain through the bag into a large bowl. Discard the pulp remaining in the jelly bag. Measure the strained juice and return it to the pan with 450 g/1 lb sugar for each 600 ml/1 pint of juice.
3 Heat gently, stirring, until the sugar has dissolved, then boil rapidly until setting point is reached (*see* page 121). Pot into jars and cover.

BEETROOT CHUTNEY

700 g/1 ½ lb cooking apples, peeled and chopped
2 large onions, peeled and chopped
1.25 ml/¼ tsp freshly ground black pepper
10 ml/2 tsp salt
5 ml/1 tsp ground ginger
2.5 ml/½ tsp ground cinnamon
pinch of ground mace
300 ml/10 fl oz malt vinegar
1.4 kg/3 lb cooked beetroot
225 g/8 oz sugar

METHOD

1 Put the apples and onions in a large stainless steel pan with the spices and vinegar and cook until tender.
2 Cut the beetroot into dice and add to the pan with the sugar. Heat gently, stirring until the sugar has dissolved, then bring to the boil and cook for 10-15 minutes, until the chutney is thick. Pot into jars and cover with vinegar-proof lids.

SPICY APPLE CHUTNEY

1.4 kg/3 lb cooking apples, peeled and chopped
225 g/8 oz onions, chopped
450 g/1 lb tomatoes, skinned and chopped
1.1 kg/2 ½ lb brown sugar
450 g/1 lb seedless raisins, chopped
100 g/4 oz currants
5 ml/1 tsp ground cloves
25 g/1 oz stem ginger, chopped
1.25 ml/¼ tsp cayenne pepper
15 ml/1 tbsp salt
900 ml/1 ½ pints malt vinegar

METHOD

1 Put the apples in a large stainless steel pan with a little water and cook until tender.
2 Add all the remaining ingredients and simmer gently for 1 ½ hours. Pot into jars and cover with vinegar-proof lids.

PICCALILLI

450 g/1 lb small courgettes, sliced
900 g/2 lb cauliflower florets
350 g/12 oz green beans, sliced and de-stringed, if necessary
450 g/1 lb small pickling onions, skinned
½ large cucumber, peeled and diced
300 g/10 oz salt
175 g/6 oz sugar
1.2 litres/2 pints white distilled vinegar
45 ml/3 tbsp plain flour
30 ml/2 tbsp turmeric
40 g/1 ½ oz mustard powder
20 g/¾ oz ground ginger

METHOD

1 Place a layer of vegetables in a large glass or ceramic bowl and cover with a good sprinkling of salt. Continue to layer vegetables and salt until all the vegetables are used. Cover the bowl and leave to stand for 24 hours.
2 The next day, drain the liquid from the vegetables that has resulted from the salting, then rinse the vegetables under cold running water to remove any undissolved salt.
3 Place the vegetables in a large stainless steel pan and add the sugar and 900 ml/1 ½ pints of the vinegar. Bring to the boil and simmer for about 15-20 minutes, until the vegetables are tender but still crisp.
4 Blend the flour and spices with the remaining vinegar, add to the pan and stir. Increase the heat and allow to boil briskly for no more than 3 minutes.
5 Spoon into jars, filling each jar to within 12 mm/½ in of the top. Screw on vinegar-proof lids while the pickle is still hot and leave to cool.

IRISH COFFEE

Serves 1

15 ml/1 tbsp Irish whiskey
5 ml/1 tsp sugar
strong black coffee
15-30 ml/1-2 tbsp double cream

METHOD
1 Pour the whiskey into a small warmed goblet and add the sugar.
2 Fill to within 12 mm/½ in of the top with black coffee and stir quickly to dissolve the sugar.
3 Top with a 6mm/¼ in layer of double cream. The best way to do this is to hold a spoon over the coffee and gently pour the cream over the back of the spoon so that the cream floats on the top of the coffee. Do not stir the cream into the coffee.

DEDICATION

*In memory of our mother, May McCann-Hunniford, and dedicated to our children who continue
to survive on our cooking*

Gloria Hunniford & Lena Cinnamond

ACKNOWLEDGEMENTS

The publishers would like to thank the following for providing
materials for photography.

The Pine Mine, London, Norman Blackburn Prints & Lithographs, London
and Somerset House of Iron, London, for the dresser that appears on the cover.

RECIPE NOTES

All spoon measurements are level.

Margarine in pastry and cake recipes refers to block margarine.

The very young, the elderly, pregnant women and anyone with immune-system problems should not eat
raw or lightly cooked eggs because of the risk of salmonella.

INDEX

Page numbers in italics refer to illustrations